IN OUTER PLACES

Adventures with Frank C. Hibben

IN OUTER PLACES

Adventures with Frank C. Hibben

Eleanor B. Hibben

Sunstone Press
Santa Fe, New Mexico

DEDICATION

To my father, Dr. Charles H. Brown, from whom I inherited my love of nature.

First Edition
Printed in the United States of America

Library of Congress Cataloging in Publication Data:

Hibben, Eleanor B., 1898-
In outer places: touring with Frank Hibben.

Includes index.
1. Hibben, Frank C. (Frank Cummings), 1910- . 2. Hibben, Eleanor B., 1898- . 3. Archaeologists—United States—Biography. 4. Archaeologists' wives—United States—Biography. 5. Voyages and travels. I. Title.
CC115.H53H53 1983 910.4 [B] 83-18293

ISBN: 0-86534-037-4 (hardcover)
ISBN: 0-86534-028-5 (softcover)

Published in 1983 by
Sunstone Press
Post Office Box 2321
Santa Fe, New Mexico 87504-2321 / U.S.A.

CONTENTS

PREFACE

One day, a woman came up to me on the street and said, "You are Dr. Hibben's wife, aren't you? You know, your husband doesn't look like an archaeologist."

From that day on, we have idly wondered just what an archaeologist should look like.

Strangely enough, archaeology and big game hunting are closely linked in our lives. No matter what continent we are camping on, somehow, when Frank starts hunting, he returns with an arrowhead, a spear point, a prehistoric utensil or some pottery.

During the war, he was aide to Admiral Foy in the Joint Chiefs of Staff in Washington and, with a rented home in Chevy Chase, I said triumphantly, "Well, you are now in a place where you can't find Indian relics."

How wrong I was. While fixing up a pen for our two dogs in the yard, he walked into the house with a grin on his face holding out an arrowhead.

When I married Frank, I was all set to be a naturalist's wife. Frank had spent most of his teenage summers in the field collecting for the Cleveland Museum of Natural History, and a year in the fields of Arizona and New Mexico living with the paid mountain lion hunters studying the mountain lion for the American Nature Association — a study which produced his master's degree in biology, a scientific report for the Smithsonian Institution and helped in the fight to save our vanishing mountain lions. So I thought I had it made.

Was I mistaken! After we lost our son in a tragic airplane

accident in Alaska, Frank accepted a year-long grant from the Ford Foundation to work in Greece and thereabouts and to finish a book on prehistoric man in Europe. During that time, he announced his intention of going on an African safari. Some years before, he had not been able to go when Dr. Crile of Cleveland had offered him a job on his own African safari to study the circulation system of giraffes (how does blood pump up that long neck?). He was in the midst of a Princeton year and his parents wouldn't let him go. Well, now the cost was not prohibitive since we were already in Greece, so off we went.

Frank was an outstanding shot and he had provided us with deer, elk, ducks and so forth for years, but now he was in seventh heaven. I don't like killing, so I made a place for myself keeping notes, studying birds (my hobby) and taking movies of live creatures — which I had already been doing in our national parks for several years. Some of these were sold and we worked for Walt Disney for two years when he started his nature series.

For ten years, we worked at obtaining certain African animals which were in danger of becoming extinct, ones suited to New Mexico's semi-desert climate. As a result there are larger herds of Barbary sheep, gemsbok, Iranian ibex, Siberian ibex, etc., freely roaming wild areas of New Mexico.

This book grew out of all these years of working and traveling, collecting and writing. It is the story, I suppose, of a reluctant huntress and, as such, tells both sides of the tale — the hunter and the hunted — and the one who sat and watched.

PART I

IN ALASKA

CHAPTER 1
On The Watery Trail Of Ancient Man

The boat lay tilted at an oblique angle in the shallow water. An eerie haze gave a feeling of unreality as the sifting rain softened the steep timbered slopes of the inlet on either side. We stood stock still at the water's edge, gazing in unbelief. Our summer home was in dire trouble.

It all began in the summer of 1941 when Frank decided to go to Alaska to work out the route of the first humans entering our continent from Siberia thousands of years ago. We did not want to leave our young daughters, Norrie aged 17 and Peggy aged 14, at home alone for the entire summer. Besides, they were old enough not only to be real companions but also to appreciate and benefit by our adventures. Since Frank had heard of an ancient site in Cook's Inlet, he decided we should charter a small boat and work our way up along the coast before starting down the Yukon. We had traveled the scenic inside passage from Vancouver to Prince Rupert, with its submerged valleys snaking inland among snow-capped mountains like Norwegian fjords, but even more spectacular in being as yet untouched by man. This latter is no longer true as it was in 1941, due to extensive lumbering and a burgeoning population with pleasure boats. However, there are thousands of miles of waterway still to be enjoyed in solitude.

Our spirits were dampened slightly when we could discover no captain who would be willing to make the trip from Glacier Bay west of Juneau, up through the Gulf of Alaska. This trip required a high insurance rate - which in itself was an ominous sign. Or it would require a boat much larger than we could afford to charter. Being landlubbers, we never gave a thought to the fact that these precautions spelled DANGER.

We finally chartered an old ex-cannery tender called the Junior. It was 72 feet long and had an extra heavy hull to safely navigate stormy waters with occasional ice. Then we found out about the summer camp in Mt. McKinley National Park where the girls could stay while we went on the rugged exploratory part of the trip down the Yukon River.

Sailing from Seattle, we worked our way northward through the spectacular inland passage, so very like the famous Norwegian fjords. The jagged snow crested Coast Range beckoned us to make a side trip up one of the long winding fjords. We decided on Bute Inlet, one of the most rugged and wild inlets, and were slowly chugging up its tortuous channel with silvery waterfalls snaking down perpendicular cliffs into the salt chuck, the background of lush green forests painting a picture of untouched beauty as we headed toward the snowy peaks at the head of the inlet. Approaching the end, we spotted tiny white mountain goats feeding in meadows high up among the snowfields.

At the very end of the inlet, we anchored the Junior and, in the rain that now began to fall, we coaxed our wheezing dinghy up the silty river. Equipped in our hip-high rubber boots and hooded rain parkas, we slipped ashore in the canoe to explore the raging river that somehow worked its way through the Coast Range to empty into the salt water. Up along an old logging road we hiked and found black bears feeding in small berry patches. One big bear spotted us, got up on a stump on his hind legs and let us admire the white crescent on his throat. Then he deliberately sank down and slipped away among the bushes. Tracks of grizzlies in the tidal mud flats made us hesitate about taking the girls farther along. We could find no trout pools in the cascading milky silt-filled river, so we returned to the canoe and started back for the Junior.

Ahead of us lay the Junior on its side on the sand flat. What had happened? As we speeded up our paddling and got within hailing distance, we saw the captain leaning forlornly out of the pilot house window. He told us that while he was taking a nap, the wind came up and the anchor dragged on the gravel bottom. Fortunately, he told us, the tide had turned and would soon float the Junior.

Frank climbed up the slippery side of the boat with a rope thrown down to him and then he helped the rest of us scramble and squirm up the side. Thoughts of refuge from the cold and rain were immediately blasted when we reached the deck. The stove and heating were out of commission as long as the boat lay on its side. The wind rose and we shivered forlornly trying to get into the main cabin.

We soon discovered that listing boats are most impractical. There was nothing to hang on to, no flat surface to walk on. We were reduced to crawling on hands and knees. No chair was level and even the sofa was untenable at such an angle. So, we sat on the floor, miserable, and huddled against the slanting cabin wall.

We heard a strange gurgling sound. Frank found the porthole in the tiny bathroom was open and the rising tide was pouring water into the opening. There was no way of closing the window, so we busied ourselves trying to save some of our belongings from the flood.

It took five hours for the tide to rise enough to straighten the boat. What a divine feeling it was when we felt a small shudder and the Junior began to float softly erect.

It was late afternoon before we sailed back down the inlet and anchored for the night by an old Indian village. The rain was pouring down now in sheets, but Frank and I went ashore to talk to a few loggers who were camped there and to an old Indian woman making a basket. We bought her unfinished basket and another old, battered but picturesque bowl for our museum, and returned once more to our now-warm home.

Next morning we slept late. We stopped at Church House to see the village while waiting for the tide to change so we could get through the Yuculta Rapids. A police boat followed us in and we learned that a party the previous evening had ended in a quarrel, and a man lay on his back on the beach with the top of his head blown off.

Nearby were two chairs, placed like a game of Going to Jerusalem. It looked like some sort of duel. Such is the authority of the Northwest Mounted Police in these regions that, after photographing the scene and taking evidence from the audience, they walked quietly out on the dock and boarded their boat for a final talk with the young prisoner and the chief of the tribe. Justice is efficient and expeditious in these parts.

A few days later, after visiting various Indian villages in all stages of disintegration, we learned that the village of Karlukwees had some totem poles still standing and also some enormous potlatch bowls. Slowly and carefully working our way between beds of kelp — the captain grouching about screwy people who wanted to go to uncharted islands — we finally anchored in a small bay in front of a dilapidated village. One beautiful totem pole stood in front of the huge barnlike potlatch house and another lay sloping toward the beach where it had fallen to rot in the mossy bank. Huge upright poles of other former houses stood as skeletons of past glory No one was in sight.

Working our way up through tropically lush bushes, we peeked into the potlatch house which still had a roof and glimpsed through the cracks in the door, a few huge carved and painted bowls. They made Frank eager to get inside.

Tom Smith of the Seaweed Clan took us to his brother's house to see potlatch vessels which he kept under his house out of the rain. These were in perfect condition, with huge spoons fitting inside them. We appreciated their desire to keep them but mourned the fact that later on their children would either let them rot, like pieces of other bowls we saw lying around in the bushes, or destroy them.

Then we met Mike Seaweed, owner of the standing totem pole. The paint was washing away in the woodpecker's eye at the top of the pole which had recently held a bird's nest, but otherwise it was weathering the rain very well.

Tom did find a mask with movable jaws and decorated with strips of blankets, mica and copper. We bought this for our museum. Mike agreed to sell the totem pole since he had no children to leave it to and since it would go to a museum and be well taken care of. We bought this for our museum at the University of New Mexico — it cost us $200 (Canadian).

I had the easy task of photographing the process, watching the men dig a three-foot hole around the base of the totem. An

Indian climbed to the roof of the potlatch house to secure the block and tackle from the boat, and the pole was lowered slowly to the ground. Afterward, it was rolled down the slope into the water.

We towed the pole behind the boat into Johnstone Straits and anchored in Beaver Cove. Here we took notes on the painting of the pole in case the salt water destroyed some of it. We could repaint it at home later on.

Luckily, the next day was calm and the water smooth as glass, an unusual state of affairs for that stretch of water. But the three days following were rough and our boat rolled from side to side as the pole zigzagged across our wake and plunged under the rising waves only to rise again and wallow sluggishly behind us. Porpoises appeared at our bow and dived back and forth and we lay on our stomachs and peered down at their glistening backs and pure white throats. As we chugged along, the porpoises leaped and dived and turned on their sides to look up at us with their friendly black eyes. I tried in vain to get some good movies of these delightful playmates.

Our arrival at Ketchikan was uneventful as was the business of obtaining customs clearance and permits and arranging to have the pole hauled back to the states on a freighter to start it on its way to our campus. Then, we headed north again to search for the routes of early man from Alaska to North America proper.

A day in Glacier Bay was a thrill, working our way among icebergs to watch Muir Glacier calve and its thunderous chunks roar down into the water as they melted along the face of the glacier. Humpback whales rolled on the surface and leaped out into the air, plunging back again with an enormously loud splash. The panorama of the snow-covered Fairweather Range to the west came out from under its cloud cover at sunset for one of its rare appearances, in spite of its name.

There is a joke in this part of Alaska that Captain Cook saw this range of jagged snowy mountains on a clear day, so he called it the Fairweather Range. It has rarely been clear since, so anyone who has seen this majestic sight without a complete cloud cover has been fortunate indeed. To us, it was a fairy tale event, unbelievably beautiful. A bank of purple clouds hung above the mountains while the pink glow of late sunlight tinted the white glaciers. In the foreground, the deep waters of the bay were deep blue and in the distance a whale leaped clear of the water arching in mid air as he disappeared into the depths with a last flip of his forked tail.

Before leaving these sheltered waters for the open Pacific, we decided to take another day in a nearby bay to fish. We netted crabs, which skittered over the bottom of the rowboat to the accompaniment of squeals from the girls as they lifted their feet out of the way of the crabs' claws. Norrie, after catching her third ugly, prickly sculpin, swore she would never fish again. To cap it off, she hooked a flounder and was gleefully pulling it in when a halibut came along and gobbled it up. Her interest in fishing ceased abruptly.

As we entered the open Pacific long before dawn, to avoid the waves that usually are whipped up by the wind, the boat began to roll. We were enjoying sleeping on deck in our sleeping bags and rubber mattresses, but the Pacific roll put an end to this. For a while we watched the Fairweather Range from the ocean side in the moonlight, but as the waves grew higher and higher, our bags began to slither back and forth across the deck and suddenly, with one monstrous wave, Norrie nearly slid under the rail. That ended our sleep for the night for even in our bunks, the incessant rolling kept us awake. Morning found us in the same state and we — one and all — kept to our bunks and went without breakfast.

When we entered the notoriously rough waters of the Gulf of Alaska, we were initiated into the unwelcome acquaintance of the famous williwaws — the unpredictable winds of Alaska. There is a notable lack of safe harbors in these parts too, and the captain began to study the charts to find some place to anchor until the sea calmed.

Fair weather still held as we gazed awestruck at ten o'clock that night at the silvery mass of Mt. St. Elias and its sister snow-shrouded peaks. Then on into the Gulf of Alaska itself.

We entered the Gulf where a storm had developed and the captain decided it was the better part of valor to find a snug harbor. But there was no such place nearby.

As we approached the little island of Kayak, the captain spied a small fishing boat anchored in the lee in an indentation that served as a possible harbor. We headed for it and found, to our dismay, that the wind seemed to circle the island and leave no sheltered spot.

The captain decided to drop the anchors and we all hoped for the best. Sleep was impossible. We couldn't stay in our berths. Even when we lay on the floor, we skidded back and forth. Frank sat at the window above his bunk and studied the shoreline of Kayak. There wasn't a break in the line of cliffs and certainly no beach to land on. What could we do in an emergency?

Just then, with a snap, an anchor cable broke. The boat swung around, the captain tried to keep her headed into the wind. He kept the engines going slow and sure, as an added precaution. The fishing boat had now disappeared.

Frank got out the life preservers and we put them on, even though in that icy, glacier-fed water we would not have had much of a chance.

About the middle of the night, we heard another crack: the second anchor gone. Then with a sickening thud, the Junior lurched violently, throwing us all down. The boat was hung up on a submerged rock and with every wave, we held our breaths, hoping it might lift us up and over the rock. However, when the wave receded, a sickening bump jarred us to our innards. This could not go on indefinitely, but the storm showed no sign of lessening. We were so tired of hanging on now that I, myself, began to feel that nothing mattered.

Gradually, the bumps got less shattering and the captain's tension lessened. We were lucky again. As had been the case in Bute Inlet, the tide was waxing and not waning — so we were hopeful it would rise soon enough to save us.

An hour passed. Now we barely scraped the tip of the hidden rock. Another hour — we floated free. The last anchor had by now snapped but the steady engine chugged along and we left Kayak Island behind us and headed for Cordova.

Never have I been so happy to slip into a snug, safe harbor and know that we weren't totally at the mercy of the elements. We were not upset to lose a few precious days inspecting the boat, repairing damage and restocking some broken dishes. We took hikes ashore up the old ore railroad, eating thimbleberries and unwinding after our ordeal.

By the time we reached Seward, at the upper end of an 18-mile inlet, we had had enough. Little did we know what lay ahead. Frank still wanted to cross Cook Inlet to see his archaeological site. On the chart it looked safe in comparison to the open gulf, so we girls gave in, as usual, to his enthusiasm.

However, as we approached the dock at Seward, we realized that this was no snug harbor. The town lies at the end of an 18-mile long inlet through which the wind roars as if it were a wind tunnel built specifically for this purpose.

The waves grew higher as we neared the dock. The captain threw a rope ashore to a waiting man only to find that the boat, riding up and down on the rope, would saw it in two. Next, he rigged a hitch to hold us out from the dock to prevent being banged unmercifully against it. And so went our dreams of a peaceful night ashore and possibly even a movie. There was no chance to leap across the seething gulf of water that leered at us between the Junior and that wonderfully secure dock.

All night the storm raged. A naval supply boat had to leave the dock and anchor in mid-inlet to ride it out. We rode out the gale and, waiting an extra day and champing at the bit as our charter was running out, we departed for Cook Inlet.

We rounded the entrance point of land and found the heavy rollers were still so boisterous that our boat was again threatened. The heavy sofa began to slide across the cabin and we feared that, with its weight, it could crash through the walls of the cabin. Regretfully, we turned back to our unwelcome anchorage at Seward.

The following day was stormy and with no sign of a letup so we decided to hire a taxi and drive the short distance to Kenai Lake and make the acquaintance of "Alaska Nellie" Lawing. Nellie had a log cabin in a spectacular setting on the very edge of a lake surrounded by massive snow-flecked mountains. She had built a small museum full of relics from her early days in Alaska during the gold rush. As we chatted, a bell tinkled at a window facing the lake. Nellie calmly got up, went to the window and pulled in a fishline with a wriggling trout at the end — a new method of fishing without wasting time. The trout bit the hook and announced its presence as it pulled on the line and started the bell ringing.

Nellie's museum held the largest moose head on record, according to Nellie, and a bear skin of a brown bear that had broken Nellie's wrist and chewed her knee before her six shots killed him. He was a special trophy because he had killed her pet black bear. The museum also displayed her revolver with half a notch in the handle — she had shot a holdup man but had not killed him — and a piano from Dawson with 20 bullet holes in it.

We learned that the train which ran back and forth from Fairbanks to Seward in two days, taking a night's rest in between at Curry, always stopped so that the passengers could get off at Lawing to see Nellie and her museum — at a small fee. That train no longer services that route.

We made arrangements to stay a day or two with Nellie later on when we would be on our way home on a passenger boat. No more small boats for us in that stormy region.

The next day was not quite so rough so we decided to try again for Cook Inlet. We put life jackets on the girls and they hung braced between the two hand rails of the steps on the "poop deck," as Frank called it. He also riled the captain by calling it "the back veranda." We had already stowed all movable things like china and glassware and had turned the chairs on their sides on the floor.

Severe waves rolled us back and forth once more and the table, which had been screwed to the floor, ripped loose and began lunging like a wild horse. This was serious. It took over an hour for the men to secure it with ropes. I expected at any moment that a sudden lurch might break an arm or a leg in the process. In the midst of this wreckage, the cherished victrola records which the girls had carefully chosen to while away the cruising tedium came loose and were crushed under the charging table.

Noontime came. We were too busy hanging on to think of being seasick. Our stomachs were hollow by this time. The cook managed to boil some water in a teakettle snuggled safely in a framework on the tiny galley stove. Eggs were boiled in the same water as the tea and bouillon. However, a great mistake was made when we peeled them. Once dropped, they bounced like rubber balls and we were busy for some time chasing eggs on hands and knees.

We had another problem swallowing the tea and bouillon. We learned that we had to swallow as the boat was rising on a wave. The sudden drop afterward was like a fast elevator and the tea wouldn't go down our throats. With the addition of dry crackers, we were able to get some nourishment.

By this time, the captain figured we couldn't get to the Bruin Bay site across Cook Inlet and we took refuge in a tiny cove which he found on his chart. The entrance was easily made and we were thrilled to see a snug bay inside. A fishing boat already anchored there had a rope stretched from fore and aft secured to the trees on the land. We followed suit.

During the night, we lost more sleep. In a snug harbor with high mountains all around, we planned on a peaceful haven. But the williwaws found us. How they could swirl over and through the mountains to funnel into that bay, we never could understand. But they did. Our boat rocked violently all night long.

As morning came the wind died down at last. We followed the fishing boat out into the open and wallowed our way across Cook Inlet. The volcanic island of Mt. Augustine rose ahead, smoking. Farther on we could see snow-covered Mt. Iliamna pouring clouds of steam out of a small side peak. With directions Frank had obtained before the trip, we anchored off a shelving beach on the south side of the inlet. Success at last. But even here, with a medium wind fighting the outgoing tide, the waves were so high that we dared not take the girls ashore with us, or even the movie camera.

I had many misgivings as we donned our life jackets and jumped into the tiny pitching dinghy, which seemed to shrink in size as it bobbed up and down on the waves. We managed to jump in as a wave lifted the dinghy toward the boat rail and then we were horrified to realize that no matter how hard Frank rowed, the famous swift-running tide of Cook Inlet was sweeping us out to sea.

The distance to shore was only a few yards, however, and

we made the gravelly beach safely. On shore, we found tracks of brown bears who seemed to be making a highway of the narrow beach on the lookout for the expected salmon run. Thankful that the bushes along the shore were not large enough to conceal a bear, we began to explore for signs of ancient man. And we found them.

A deeply buried hearth gave evidence of ancient fires along the shore and many chipped implements lay scattered about.

So, it must have been that man, migrating across the once-dry Bering Straits, found his way here. Mammoth bones and three flint points used by the ancient hunters were all the proof we needed.

As we looked out across the still uninhabited, unfriendly reaches of land around us, we felt sorry for these rugged ancient newcomers.

Perhaps they were a small band exploring on their own, or somehow they were separated from their fellows during hunting, for the main route lay much farther north in more favorable level country. Surely then, as now, they would have had to return the way they came to get around the Mt. McKinley barrier, or the water of Cook Inlet (which extends far north of where we were) or even the wide Yukon.

After doing some digging, during which I did more watching for bears than excavating or collecting, we began to wonder how we would ever get back on the Junior. She rode enticingly near, close enough that we could shout back and forth. But the waves and current in between were terrifying.

Obeying the captain's orders, we towed the dinghy toward the head of the inlet, trudging along till we were well upriver from the Junior. This would allow time to diagonal across the current and reach the Junior before being swept past. If we didn't make it, we would be swept out into Cook Inlet. We went much farther than we first decided, as the prospect of a watery and cold interlude didn't appeal. At long last we hopped into the bobbing boat and Frank rowed as hard as he could. The boat swept along faster than we thought possible. The Junior looked farther away every minute. I hung on for dear life. The captain leaned far over the rail ready to catch the rope I had in my hands as we rushed by. I am no expert rope thrower. Suppose I fouled it up or caught the rope on something in throwing it. I gritted my teeth and fixed my eyes on the nearing Junior.

Frank gave a gigantic haul on the oars and the tiny dinghy swept against the welcome side of the Junior. I tossed the rope — the captain caught it. The rushing tide swirled us dizzily around so that we hit the Junior with a crash. We grabbed the rail and hauled ourselves aboard.

"That was a close call," mumbled Frank. It was lucky we hadn't taken the movie camera. We were drenched.

A very relieved captain started the engines and hauled up the anchor. This in itself was quite a trick.

From the look on the captain's face, he was already headed for home. He couldn't get back to Seattle fast enough to get rid of us — and go back to safe waters in the inland passage. We realized, by this time, why the insurance rates on boats going through the Gulf of Alaska were so high.

Then, cruising swiftly toward open water, there was a grinding crunch and the Junior's bow rose sickeningly in the air. Not again. The stern swirled in the current and the grinding increased. We all got boat hooks to probe whatever was grounding us. A hasty look at the chart showed no underwater reef. It was just one of those many uncharted rocks which abound in Alaska.

What to do? The hooks met no obstacles, no firm place on which to push the Junior free. We were helpless. The shore was less forbidding than Kayak Island and there were fishermen here who might be willing to help.

Another look at the tide chart brought a sigh of partial relief from the captain. The tide was rising. It might float us off. And that it did. The grinding slowly eased and within a few minutes — which seemed like hours — we floated free.

"Was your darned archaeological find worth all this?" mumbled the captain.

"Yes, it was," replied Frank. "You'll hear more about it some time."

The captain remained unconvinced.

Our return to Seward was rough and uneventful but, as if to give a parting reminder that we were in dangerous country, Alaska gave us one last thrill.

The JUNIOR left high and dry by the wind and tide in the British Columbia inlet of Bute.

Right: Hasselborg standing in the doorway of his cabin. He always seemed to wear his hat and binoculars.

Below: Hasselborg threw his hat at the charging brown bear.

Opposite Top: Norrie (left) and Peggy en route to Alaska on the Junior.

Opposite Bottom: The Pack train having difficulty crossing the swift Muskwa River.

We were tied up to the dock where heavy machinery was being loaded onto a freighter. There was much noise and bustle and I looked out the porthole to see what the new thundering was. The piles were swaying back and forth like eel grass.

"Frank," I cried. "Why don't they make these docks stronger in this stormy country?"

Frank looked up and the girls gave a cry of surprise. The piling was swaying dizzily. Mercy! The whole dock was falling down! We'd better cast loose and escape. We looked up the street of Seward. Several buildings were also swaying crazily and the street looked like a writhing snake.

An earthquake.

It was, fortunately, a small one — a parting gesture at the end of an exciting adventure on the watery trail of ancient man.

CHAPTER 2
Hasselborg & The Bears

Our sixty-foot chartered boat felt its way into Mole Harbor on Admiralty Island, Alaska. The tide is very strong here and at low tide a boat can't even get in, as most of the harbor is a mass of seaweed at this time. We got out our binoculars to look at a cabin at the mouth of the river that emptied into the harbor. There stood Allen Hasselborg, hermit, dear friend, bear man. He looked the same as he had the last time we had seen him except that his black spade beard had some gray in it. His familiar canvas hat was on his head (probably with its knot of black jack gum stuck to the top for future use) and his spotting scope hung around his neck.

Hasselborg did not know we were coming and he wanted to make sure he wanted whatever it was coming toward him. He is very touchy about who lands on his island and disturbs his bears. He takes his motor dinghy about twice a year to Juneau to return library books and to renew his own stock, for he is a voracious reader. So, naturally, letters do not reach him at any specific time. He also takes his marten and beaver skins to sell in order to have money to buy provisions.

As we waved to him from the foredeck, he recognized us and, with a broad smile, he walked down the path to the beach to welcome us.

We never asked questions about Hasselborg's past, although we had heard rumors of an unhappy love affair in his home state of Florida and we knew he had driven a stagecoach in Arizona for some time before he got to Alaska. Upon reaching Admiralty Island, he never left it again, as far as we know. He built his cabin (which today stands in ruins), put in a large vegetable garden and vainly tried to fence out the deer who enjoyed his lettuce. He was a prodigious reader and was well-versed in everything going on in the world. But Hasselborg spent no time worrying about what he was missing.

When we came ashore, he made us right at home. His cabin was divided into four parts even though it was only one room: kitchen, dining room, bedroom and sitting room. And woe be unto the person who took a plate of food into the living room!

The girls left us to go fishing but returned disappointed. Not a nibble. Hasselborg got up, took his pole, hook and a piece of bacon and told the girls to follow him. Soon a huge silvery dolly varden was flashing on the bank. Thereupon, he taught the girls the tricks he knew and every time they came back to the cabin, there was plenty of fish for supper.

Later, we went out to look for his famous bears. He had lived there so many years and had never had any trouble around his cabin. Most of the bears nearby were his friends and he named them Dark Pants, Brown Pants, Sinbad, Inbad, Blondie and he knew which ones he could trust and which to watch out for. He knew the old patriarchs who were shy and minded their own business and the young bucks who were trouble makers.

When a young deer came along and jumped the fence into his garden, Hasselborg shooed her out with a mild scolding. When an array of bears came to look for the salmon which had not yet begun to run, he acted differently.

Often I wondered why the brown bears of Europe and Asia could be tamed enough to dance in rhythm in circuses and yet our own brown bears who resemble them physically (including the humps on their shoulders) seemed to be untamable and ferocious. They all looked alike on the surface.

On one rainy day, we slogged ashore and established a blind for our movie camera in a clump of willows on a tiny island at the mouth of a river entering Swan Cove.

As usual, the bears appeared to fish for the salmon which were beginning their run upriver. Hasselborg lay down, put his hat over his face and began to snore. How did he know it was safe? For quite a time I sat enthralled, watching the antics of the bears. There were so many salmon that the bears had their fill and were soon bored and pawing around for something to do with their spare time.

One of them stalked out into the shallows, caught a struggling salmon, tossed it into the air and then sat down on it. He then reached around underneath his bottom and hauled it out, and tossed it into the air again.

Some bald eagles came down on the beach to nibble on scraps of salmon discarded by the bears and the young bears began to play a game of tag with them. It was endlessly amusing and provided us with excellent pictures.

Finally, after a few hours, I took out my accordion. It was time to try an experiment I had in mind. A young female was playing with a fish on the opposite bank. When I picked up the instrument, Hasselborg sat up, wide awake. He didn't like the look of that female. I took up the accordion anyway and began to play *Oh, Susanna.*

The bear pricked up her ears and looked in our direction.

Then she shook her head as if to clear her ears. The music continued. She growled. Then suddenly, she turned her back to us and tore huge chunks of sod from the bank and tossed them around. As the minutes passed, she became so upset that Hasselborg suggested I stop playing. Thus, this unmusical bear acquired the name of Susanna.

Before I could put up the accordion, however, Susanna became unreasonably angry. She turned and came right for us, head down in the classic manner of a charging brown bear. She couldn't see us but that made no difference; she came within about fifteen feet of us.

Hasselborg stood up and told us to do the same. That startled her. Then, as she came closer, we began to kick water in her face. That certainly had never happened to her before and it provided an excuse for her to gracefully withdraw into the woods, grumbling as she went.

From that time on, the men heckled me about my disastrous experiment and made unfriendly remarks about my musical ability. My theory that these bears would respond to music like their European cousins did was destroyed.

Returning to our skiff at dusk — about nine o'clock — was

a risky business as the tide had gone way out and our boat was not only on the far side of the harbor, but stranded on gravel.

Susanna had disappeared but other bears were slipping out to catch salmon before dusk. We gathered up the camera and tripod and Frank's gun (which he carried with solid ball ammunition in case we got into trouble at close quarters), and Hasselborg led the way with his ancient rusty gun, which we doubted would work since he hadn't fired it in years.

As we walked along the edge of the shore, a safe distance from the deep forest, I turned to look back at Frank. I nearly dropped my camera in amazement, for not 25 feet behind him stood a huge brownie on his hind feet, looking over us.

He stood taller than Frank and I found myself looking up at him. Frank turned and when he raised his gun it seemed to be pointing skyward.

I nudged Hasselborg who turned around and took in the situation. Then he calmly walked on.

"That is just old Dark Pants, he mumbled. "He's just curious." At which, the bear dropped to all fours, curiosity assuaged, and disappeared in the tall grass on the beach.

As we neared our boat, we were horrified to see another bear between us and the boat. We went back toward the woods to walk around the bear. I suddenly realized my film had run out when I got the picture of Dark Pants behind Frank. Those were the days of black and white film, and I had to sit down on a slimy rock and put my arms up to the elbows inside the black loading bag (with the camera inside) in order to change films by feel.

If the bear had charged me at that moment, I would have been a sitting duck and I was especially nervous trying to change the film, watching the bear, my hands trembling and making a funny clattering sound from inside the bag.

The bear looked at me curiously. Then Frank and Hasselborg attracted his attention and drew his interest away.

By now the boat was only about 100 yards away but the bear was right in between us. He started that slow deliberate walk of a charging bear, swinging his head from side to side.

Hasselborg took off has canvas hat with its topknot of gum and threw it at the bear.

It hit the bear's face and he stopped at the curious smell, not just of a human but of the licorice gum.

He sniffed it and began to nuzzle the gum. This was an insult to Hasselborg who really cherished that gum. He forgot his admonitions to us never to throw a rock at a bear, stooped over and picked up a rock and threw it.

The rock hit the bear on the nose and it started to bleed.

Hasselborg said to get in the boat as quickly as possible. We walked around the bear and reached the boat while Hasselborg lingered, trying to figure out how to get his beloved hat and gum back. Fortunately, the bloody nose made the bear think twice, and he pretended he had business in the woods and, very slowly and with great dignity, the bear walked away from us.

We had a hard time dragging the boat to deeper water but we managed. We stayed on the boat and Hasselborg returned to his cabin. We never could get him to sleep on the boat with us or to take longer trips to other inlets, for he loved his cabin.

When it came time to say goodbye, we were very sad. He was getting older by now and the next time we saw him he had a snow white beard and was contemplating moving to a retirement home at Sitka for old timers.

Hasselborg lived several more years. It was on a trip after the 1957 one with friends that we found him on the dock at Juneau waiting to go to Sitka, a sad ending for such an active independent life.

But we still keep a corner of our affections dedicated to our dear old friend Allen Hasselborg.

CHAPTER 3
Muskeg, Mountains & Nightmares

The huge log snapped and crackled as the flames wavered and caught on the side branches. I squirmed in the sand to make a hollow for my hip to rest in. The warmth of the fire relaxed me for a few moments, but a biting cold wind chilled my back. I turned over. Perhaps by hunching up like a baby I could keep my stomach warm and let the fire take care of my backside. As I turned, I noted the hunched figures of Frank and our three friends.

The airplane, a float-equipped Beaver, was a shadowy form just beyond. The pilot, Ralph, had chosen to stay in the doubtful protection of the cabin for the night.

We were stranded on remote Chesterfield Lake in northern British Columbia without food or sleeping bags.

The story of how we got there goes back to 1950 when we took a rugged pack trip north of the Prophet River and along the Muskwa — famous for prize Stone sheep. Our guide Rhenie Dhenin proved excellent, and his assistant Art McLean was tops. Around a campfire one night, Art had told of working during the war in a primitive area never before explored, bulldozing a road for Hitler to invade Canada — as preposterous as that may seem.

There were no authentic maps of this country and the idea that it might prove virgin territory for a big game hunt was irresistible to Frank. The more he thought about it, the more he wanted to go there.

After hours of discussion on evenings around the campfire, Rhenie and Art decided that it might be feasible. It would take many more horses to pack extra food and supplies and they would have to start out a month in advance of us to cut their way through the wilderness. Muskeg is the worst enemy of this kind of trip. The one we were on was a nightmare as far as Lois, our cook, and I were concerned. There was never a good way around these swamps and the floundering horses, sometimes screaming in terror, were nerve-wracking. One horse had already been killed by an old tree stub which pierced his stomach in the muskeg. Often Lois and I got off and mucked through it.

Four years later the trip was actually taking place. We found kindred souls in Harry Combs (now president of Lear Jet), a rancher friend of his, Vance Thornburg, and university professor Wayne Eubank. We had our pack outfit and the plan was for us to start a month after the pack train, fly to Watson Lake in the Yukon, charter a plane to take us to Chesterfield Lake — a pinpoint on the map — where we would meet the pack train. Then we would walk out toward the Alcan Highway, hunting as we went. It sounded simple.

We started with great enthusiasm from Watson Lake, thrilled to see so much wilderness below us with no sign of any trail except game trails. At first, pilot Ralph knew the snow and glacier-topped mountains and river valleys, but soon we were studying the map and following strange river valleys.

As we flew, the mountains became higher and whiter and the rivers more turbulent. Even the muskeg swamps were unmarred even by game trails. This bothered us. Where was the game? No one had ever hunted here. Occasionally if we passed close to a cliff, a herd of mountain goats dotted the rocky ledges. Moose grazed in a few swamps. A bear lumbered into the protection of the forest. Hour followed hour, and my apprehension grew as the distance grew between us and any emergency help.

Ralph and Harry studied the map and began to be uneasy as we spotted several charted "lakes" that turned out to be muskeg. Whoever made the chart must have flown over in the winter when all vast expanses of snow were identified as lakes. No ground crew had ever surveyed this country. Would Chesterfield turn out to be a swamp too? No, Art had told us he had camped on Chesterfield during his bulldozing days.

Finally, when we were about to lose our nerve, the long sausage-shaped form of Chesterfield appeared ahead of us. The plane circled wider and wider. No sign of a pack train. Ralph looked at his gas gauge.

"We'll have to land or I'll be short of fuel to get out of here," he said.

We taxied uneventfully up the lake, startling a large moose which was slopping up water lilies at one side. Carefully we approached a nice gravel beach at the upper end where any pack train would first reach the lake from the pass to the south. Stepping out onto the beach, Frank spotted the tracks of an enormous grizzly.

An immediate consultation was in order. Ralph could not leave us without supplies — what if the pack train didn't arrive? And he couldn't return with the full load either because of limited gas. He figured we were nearer Fort Nelson than Watson Lake, but found over his wireless that it was socked in.

Here we discovered our first mistake. Our friends had brought their sleeping bags and duffles with them. Frank had figured it would be simpler to ship ours ahead to travel north on the horses. Now, if no pack train appeared, we were without sleeping bags. We also had no food with us except the scanty emergency rations required by law in this frontier country. For seasoned campers, this was an inexcusable mistake. It was now late afternoon so there was nothing to do but spend the night and hope Fort Nelson's weather would clear. We might be able at least to get there and regroup.

We put together our fishing rods and while the men conferred, I tried my luck from the shore of the lake. Putting a daredevil spoon on the leader, I flipped it out as far as I could. A hard tug nearly pulled me off balance as a huge trout jumped out of the water and shook his head to get free. We all shouted as the fish fought and Frank waded into the water to grab him in case he was too heavy to land without a net. We were all so hungry that we took no chances of losing our supper. The trout must have weighed at least seven or eight pounds. Frank could not stand to have his wife beat him, so he was soon rigging up another rod and almost immediately we had another monster.

In case we were stranded indefinitely, we decided to save the rations as long as possible. The men went for a short exploratory hike to locate the moose we had seen just before landing. They dragged back to the plane disheartened. So supper consisted of delicious fish and tea. Ahead of us loomed the prospect of a long, dark, cold night but at least it wasn't raining.

Few people realize how long a night can last when you're sleeping on sand and gravel with an icy wind cutting to the marrow. I don't think any of us admired the beautiful spruce-trimmed lake that rippled at our feet in rhythmical wavelets that would have soothed the ordinary sleeper. Snow-flecked mountains rose against the sky at the lower end of the lake, but we ignored them. We were too busy feeling sorry for ourselves.

I sat hunched up by the fire, musing over my adventures with Frank through the years. Never a dull moment. If he wasn't dreaming up some new adventure, his mind was exploring new fields for archaeological excavations or hunting expeditions. But this moment on the isolated gravel bar in the middle of an unmapped wilderness seemed the worst.

Morning came and with it the lowering clouds threatened us. The wireless brought us no comfort. Ralph was really worried now. He could not leave us on this forsaken beach and realized a full load would preclude having enough gas. After a great deal of thought and study of his maps, he figured that we *might* have enough gas to get to Rainbow Lake to the west — the opposite direction of where the pack train should be. However, he had left two drums of gas on the shore for emergencies two years earlier. Further, the lake was near a trapping trail and within possible reach of help.

So, with a prayer on our lips, we piled into the Beaver and took off. We gazed back at the pass, hoping for a glimpse of the missing pack train, but no movement disturbed the primaeval scene. Nothing broke the monotony of green forest. Our gas gauge slowly flickered toward empty. We held our breath, hoping to lighten the load.

Luck was with us. Rainbow Lake glistened silvery under gray skies. We lost altitude slowly and taxied along to the shore. On the bank we could see the welcome barrels tilting crazily on a mossy knoll.

However, when Ralph got out of the plane and tilted one up, it teetered back and forth: empty. Winter snows had rusted out the can and all the gas was gone. He tilted the other one apprehensively. It was full.

Studying the map, Ralph figured we did not have enough gas to reach Watson Lake, but that we might be able to make Dease Lake where the Dalziels had a summer cabin well supplied with beds and food. Dalziel was a guide himself, as well as a flier; he and his wife used this Dease Lake cabin as a headquarters in the summer. He would also have some means of communication with his own headquarters at Watson Lake. This was even farther west and farther from our lost pack train, but we had no choice.

On we flew, a little reassured by now, and soon we were circling over a large lake, then taxiing up to the dock. Not far behind the dock we could see a charming log cabin, with smoke hovering over it. My stomach finally returned to its normal position and, with a sigh, we all relaxed and smiled. Even the pack train did not concern us when a warm bed and food lay ahead.

We were welcomed by June Dalziel and were made at home in snug quarters. That first night was memorable. Homemade bread and soup followed by cake, followed by a warm bed.

However, we still had to find our pack train. This would take valuable time as it was early fall and if all had gone well, we would just now be hunting our way out of the wilderness and returning to fall semester at the university. Rhenie could take no chances of an early snow marooning his horses (which were more valuable to him than we were) in this wilderness.

After two days we were able to engage a small plane to scout the country for our pack train. The search was successful, the pack train was located on the shores of Fern Lake — several miles south of Chesterfield. It took still another day to get the Beaver again. When we finally landed beside the camp and our old friends came down to the shore to greet us, it was like old home week. One of the wranglers had brought his wife, Lois, as cook, which worked out beautifully.

We waved farewell to Ralph who must have been overjoyed to be done with us. We greeted our duffles like long lost treasures and I remember hugging my warm sleeping bag. We were most sympathetic when we learned from Rhenie the troubles they had had. The trail had long since grown over. Some of it had to be cleared of fallen timber, horses got stuck in muskeg and one day a grizzly bear had stampeded the whole outfit. And, said Rhenie finally, "Time is running out and we'll have to start back immediately.

"Can't we hunt the area before we leave?" moaned Frank. "We just saw a bunch of sheep —"

"Nothing doing," answered Rhenie. "I have a week's trail even after I leave you to be picked up by plane at Dead Man's Lake."

What an engaging name, I thought. A perfect place to end this disastrous trip.

The return was a nightmare. Rain hounded us. If you have ever made camp in the rain after huddling in a soggy saddle all day, you'll know what it was like. Unloading soggy bedrolls and duffles, laying them on the wet ground with no place to dry out, helping Lois find a few sticks of wood dry enough to start the iron stove were major problems. Hunting was almost impossible with clouds shrouding the higher mountains. Crossing and recrossing the Muskwa was a continuing vexation and poor Art was always borrowing my old reliable horse to test the depth to find where to cross.

One horse slipped in the mud and lay groaning on his side. He had to be unpacked completely before he could get up.

The muskeg was a constant threat with the horses lunging and plunging and often we dismounted to do the lunging ourselves. My horse, Archie, was the only one who was philosophical about it. He would actually stop before a big mudhole or a bad watercrossing where the boulders were rolling and grinding along the bottom of the river and would take his time, inching his way along without becoming harrassed.

One particularly gloomy morning Vance cheered us by saying in a loud voice, "Oh, goody, goody! We get to ride horses today."

That night he insisted that he was riding a three-gaited

horse — stumble, fall and back-up.

On another drizzling day, Harry spoke up, — "To think we are paying good money to be this miserable."

However, every one was a pretty good sport and, in between rains, the men did get some hunting for Stone sheep, goats, moose and even caribou. We never did figure out why there weren't any trophy animals in mountains that were unexplored by hunters except, perhaps, an occasional Indian.

Harry and Vance had to leave us a week before the end of the trip due to business, but they made arrangements with Ralph before he left us to meet them at a certain lake on a certain day. I don't know to this day how they worked it out, but it was successful. We left them on the shore of Blue Lake with food enough to get by in case of delay. Art stayed with them until the plane showed up on schedule.

Finally, typically in the rain, a few days later we slogged into the muskeg around Dead Man's Lake. A plane was to pick us up the next day to fly us out to Fort St. John.

That night while the men made camp, I took a pail to go and pick some wild cranberries. Fresh fruit would be a delectable change from our heavy meat diet.

I found a nice clump along the lake shore and sat down in my raincoat.

A noise made me jump. Bear? No — a horse came out of the pines, an Indian sat on it staring in amazement. The horse shied at the strange apparition. The Indian looked as if he were seeing a ghost and I must have looked the same.

It turned out that another hunting party had flown into the lake the week before and were camped a mile away. They had avoided the worst muskeg we had struggled in four years before.

We found we knew one of the Texans in the party; we had met him at a New Mexico dude ranch called Martin's Ranch a few years before. Hunting instead of fighting muskeg, their trophies were far better than ours. So it goes with hunting.

Nor did this end our troubles. The rain and fog continued, the days passed and no plane could get through. The men dared not hunt far from camp for fear the plane might land when they were out. There was plenty of game of all kinds nearby, but they wouldn't risk it.

By the time the plane did come, our food was running low and we had decided to give up and ride the five days to the Alcan Highway to get out. But the welcome hum of the plane's engine proved to be more than a figment of our imaginations as it taxied towards us on the gray, sullen waters of the lake.

Our troubles were still not over. When we got to Fort St. John, it seemed as if all the oilmen, miners and prospectors were leaving Alaska at once to escape being winterbound. We could get no seat on any plane at all. In the end, we took a bus to Edmonton and started home a week late.

Of all my experiences with Frank, the night on the sandbar at Chesterfield remains the most thrilling — and the most nightmarish.

PART II

IN AFRICA & INDIA

CHAPTER 4
Africa's Most Dangerous Game

The bull elephant loomed over us in the darkness.

We could see the white of his tusks in the starshine. Two prongs of ivory were so close I could have reached out and touched one. His curling trunk made sniffing sounds in the stillness as he took our scent. Ordinarily elephants run from a human odor, but this one didn't. He probably had a poisoned arrow stuck in his guts somewhere. He rumbled in his throat.

Frank, beside me, raised his large caliber rifle and pointed it upward. This was the moment of truth and a very difficult one it was. If the bull elephant even fell forward, he would crush us both.

Frank lowered the gun and dug me violently in the ribs with his stock. "Ouch!" I hissed.

You cannot run from an elephant. If we moved a hair this bull would strike with trunk or tusks or both.

Crouched in a flimsy blind beside a salt lick in the southern Sudan close to the Congo border, we had hoped that one of the rare forest-dwelling bongo would come into the lick. Instead we got a nasty-tempered bull elephant. And now Frank was courting disaster. He was standing up. The probing trunk of the bull was just above his head.

Suddenly my left leg was on fire. A hot branding iron could not have produced a sharper pain. The burning moved up my thigh. In a few seconds the flame reached my neck. Searing pain moved across my face. I brushed at the pain. Instantly my hand and arm burned with the penetration of a thousand white hot needles.

"Ants!" Frank said aloud. "Fire ants!" They were moving inside my safari pants. A thousand of them swarming over my face and eyes. In my shirt, gnawing at my arm pits.

Like two comedians doing a buck and wing onto the stage, Frank and I sidestepped and shuffled out of the blind, oblivious to the elephant. Perhaps he was astounded at the fantastic antics of these two crazy people or maybe at that instant the fire ants reached his front leg, for he turned and went away, trumpeting loudly, perhaps to clear a few ants out of his nose.

As for us, we tore off our clothes and swept handfuls of seething ants from our bodies.

Finally, Frank, with a great show of courage, ran back to the blind to get the flashlight. In its feeble beam, we picked ants off each other and shook them out of our clothes.

Braving that elephant on the Congo border (it was still the Congo in 1959) was not the only time ants proved more terrifying that any other living thing on the Dark Continent. I recall vividly at least a dozen other instances when we ignored possible annihilation by buffaloes, leopards, cobras or even the less visible danger of malaria, and succumbed to ants.

At the Long Bar in the New Stanley Hotel in Nairobi, Kenya, probably more animals are slaughtered every evening than any other spot in all of Africa. Generally, the talk centers around the "big five." These are the dangerous animals, the ones that bite back. The big five are the elephant, rhino, buffalo, lion and leopard.

Any time professional hunters proclaim the elephant as the most deadly, four others will come forward to champion another animal. Each has stories to back up his claim. I well remember the time, in an infrequent lull in the conversation, that I said clearly, "I think you are all wrong, gentlemen. The most dangerous animal in Africa is the safari ant."

Seasoned hunters turned, glasses in their hands, to stare at me. A few years ago, women were unwelcome at the Long Bar, but times have changed. Now there are a few women hunters and even a few famous photographers. Sometimes women are even allowed to say something or to recount a hunting experience — if they are not too long-winded. The independence of Kenya has wrought many wonders and the emancipation of women is one of the side benefits. But for a woman to challenge the big five was blasphemy.

Happily, my safari clothes were stained just enough, my bush jacket showing a number of tri-cornered rents where the wait-a-bit thorns had caught. At least I was no novice. Perhaps it was this, or the sheer audacity of my statement, that caused the whole room to pause in their drinking and to listen.

"Ants aren't even animals," said one man punching his neighbor in the ribs with an elbow. The fellow returned to his Pimms cup. A quiet man with a short-sleeved jacket and the bronze arms of a professional hunter assumed the leadership of the opposition.

"Why do you think an ant is more dangerous than an elephant, my good woman?" he said in a paternal tone.

"Ten thousand tiny bites are worse than one big one," I began. "Besides, ants are the only living creatures in Africa feared by one and all of the big five. I'll bet there is not one of you who has not had some painful experience with safari ants."

A mumble of ascent was heard.

In the course of many safaris in Africa, Frank and I have had many encounters with ants and the ants won every time. Snakes are a minor worry in comparison with ants and we rarely see a snake. I have been nearly stepped on by an elephant before he saw me and have been within arm's length of lions photographing them. Buffalo and rhinos have charged us repeatedly on many occasions. However, the only thing I have ever run from has been ants.

The most obvious of the African ants are the safari ants. All of them seem to march in lines, but safari ants have developed this trait into a highly organized, lethal army, feared by man and beast alike.

I thought at first that safari ants were fascinating. We saw our first migration in Kenya years ago. Our professional hunter carefully pointed out the two different-sized varieties, standing well back from the seething ribbon as they passed.

Safari ants, several million in a colony, move in a strip two or three inches wide with the smaller workers in the middle. These are the plain-looking, innocent ants of modest size. On the outer edge of the column march the larger warriors. These are about three-quarters of an inch in length. Twice as big as the workers, they are armed with a ferocious pair of pincers. At the slightest disturbance, the warriors mobilize on each side of the column and attack. Their pincers are so powerful that even the most thick-skinned animals move out of their way. Their bite is similar to a bee sting. Once the warrior closes his pincers on an enemy, he never relaxes his grip, even though his head is torn from his body. It is because of this trait that many of the African natives use these ants to suture a wound. A row of ants will keep a gaping wound closed until it is healed.

I noticed with considerable amusement a particularly belligerent elephant move out of the way when a column of safari ants headed toward one of his feet. After a train of safari ants passes, not a green leaf is left; a bare trail about six inches wide marks their passing.

Once I saw a dead bird lying on the ground ahead of one such column. Seconds later, it was a skeleton, picked clean of fiber and feather.

In southern Sudan several years ago, we had our first serious bout with safari ants. Late one afternoon, we were relaxing from a long dusty, bumpy ride and we had little water available for any purpose. We camped at the edge of the tangled underbrush near the hut of our government-recommended bongo guide, Hawash Gedde.

Hawash was quite a character — always willing to help, smiling and twitching his ragged mustache and saying "Yessessir," to every remark. His wife (or one of his wives) lived in a hut with her eleven children — and these formed the entire village. They were most hospitable, ready to share their one egg from their one hen and also to provide us with pineapples, bananas and papayas.

Our camp was settled snugly under the tall trees where small green parrots or parakeets chattered.

Ungainly hornbills lumbered by, squawking harshly and tiny monkeys appeared and disappeared in the trees.

Large gray plantain eaters with their tall pointed crests and long tails called noisily from the tree tops. No wonder they are called "Go away birds," for that is what they seemed to shout at us.

Pale blue fairy flycatchers still flitted into the air and gracefully swooped back again as they feasted on the innumerable insects.

I had taken refuge under the mosquito netting hanging over our cots. The eye bees were intolerable. These inventions of the devil abound in many parts of Africa, immune to insecticides and seemingly abundant at all times of the year. They are actually like miniature bees — the size of large gnats. They do not bite much, if at all, but they seek moisture and salt and bombard the eyes, ears, mouth and nose, crawling into the hair and down the neck. My first reaction was that any insect that did not bite could be easily endured.

But that was before I had encountered eye bees.

The abominable midgets came in myriads like the famed black flies of the Canadian wilderness. I could not even sit and read a book for so many were flitting between my eyes and the pages. We couldn't converse without taking in a mouthful as we spoke. Nor could we breathe with impunity. They even interfered with our movies, perching around the edge of the lens, clouding the air in every direction. I did find that the mosquito netting helped to strain out enough of them so that I could read, automatically squashing them as they lit on my book. On top of all this, their dead bodies have an acrid smell which grows more unpleasant as time passes.

Frank and I had retired early this first night in Zandeland, for we were to start before dawn to visit a salt lick where the bongo were supposed to appear at daylight.

Suddenly Frank's shout awakened all of us. Frank, who ordinarily could not be aroused by a burglar or even a fire, was wide awake and yelling. To me, this fact was both astounding and alarming. Then, by the light of my flashlight I saw the tent floor seething in waves of black. An army of ants had taken possession — millions, billions, trillions — a national debt of ants.

I sat crouched on my bed, not daring to move and tucked my mosquito netting closer around the edge of my mattress. I hoped that ants could not crawl up the metal legs of the cot.

Kisanga, the only camp boy who spoke English, appeared out of the night and told me not to move, to keep my netting up. Frank's infestation was caused by the netting hanging down on the floor of the tent.

He was dancing up and down in front of the tent while two boys picked each individual ant from his flesh. These ants hang on until removed one by one.

The boys grabbed hunks of still-burning wood from the last night's cooking fire and began to pull his cot from under the tent. I sat like a Buddha on my throne and watched proceedings — for once an innocent bystander. The boys shook out the linen, passing the sheet and mattress quickly over the now-blazing fire. Meanwhile the ants, their line of march disrupted, were milling around in a solid mass of black on the tent floor.

I was horrified to see the boys build a ring of fire around my tent. Was I to be burned at the stake? I called out in fear to Frank. By this time, his dancing was slowing down as fewer *siafu* clung to his skin; he looked up and saw my predicament.

"Kisanga," he shouted, "Memsahib! Be careful!"

Kisanga saw my fear and hastily assured me the fire would be kept under control. However, as the flames licked hungrily along the path of dried leaves and twigs, I longed to leap them and join Frank.

I became intrigued by the sight of the vast army of approaching ants which was turned aside by the fire to continue their march outside the camp. Beneath me, meanwhile, all was chaos. The line of march had long since been shattered and thousands of black ants were milling around in wild disorder. They couldn't get out and they couldn't find a leader.

Kisanga, standing by, assured us that the greatest danger was past and the main line of march destroyed. The worst was over. It seemed that the safari ants usually move at night and our tent just happened to be in the direct line of their march. If Frank's netting had not touched the ground, the line probably would have passed us unnoticed.

It took over an hour for the ants beneath me to re-establish their line; the leaders to crawl over the still-hot ashes and thence onward to join their main army a few yards away. The writhing line hurried over the hot ground, the stragglers finding safety in the reorganized line of march.

But it was morning before the last ants disappeared.

Thoroughly exhausted, Frank flopped down on his cot under a nearby tree and I napped fitfully in the tent.

Our worst experience was in former French Equatorial Africa on the west coast just south of the Sahara Desert. Just south but far enough for the climate to change from the dry heat of the desert to the damp enervating heat of the tropics. This was not the lush and beautiful jungle of Tarzan fame, but rather sparse trees with dried up foliage except where waterholes provided small islands of real jungle. The heat was overpowering.

Frank had sought out this uncomfortable place in the Central African Republic to hunt for the elusive giant eland, the largest of all antelopes. In spite of its size — larger than a Brahma bull — it is as shy and elusive as a bongo. How such a huge animal can remain hidden in those open woodlands is still a mystery to me.

Our camp was beside a small stream in a lush bit of jungle. Brightly colored birds sang in the leafy forest around us with mellow flute-like voices. This is the only place in the world we have visited where so many brightly colored birds have equally as many varied and enchanting voices. (The South American parrots and their kin are so noisy!) White egrets similar to ours at home and saddle-billed storks waded around in a tiny pond nearby. Saddle bills look as if they had come out of the pages of *Alice in Wonderland* — their red and yellow painted bills and pink knees "livening-up" their black and white plumage. I am an avid birdwatcher and I would have been in seventh heaven if it had not been for the steamy heat and the ever-present eye bees.

As we retired under our mosquito nets that night, perspiration streaming off our bodies, we were careless in tucking in our netting. We lay on our damp cots uncovered and miserable. Dysentery added to our misery and we were awake on and off all night long.

About the middle of the night, Frank and I were still wide awake. The now-familiar sensation of a veil being pulled across our faces — which at first feels like mosquito netting — made us wipe our eyes. This was a mistake. The ants, which had marched up our nettings and across our cots, immediately took offense and grabbed us with their pincers.

We shot out of our cots with simultaneous yells, waking up the camp. In the pitch blackness of the tropical night, I ran stumbling into the woods and tore off my night clothes.

By this time the ants were all through my hair, so I called Frank to go back and get my comb. He was in just as much misery as I but his hair was short and the ants easily dislodged. Together in the darkness, aided only by a weak flashlight, we picked off ants for a long time.

Pandemonium had broken loose. The camp boys rushed up half clothed — meaning they had shorts on. Immediately spotting the trouble, they grabbed gasoline cans and poured some in a circle around our beds. It was far too hot a night to use tents.

Soon the circle of fire enclosed our isolated beds. In the sudden illumination, I had to retire to the woods (in my state of undress) to continue to pick ants off Frank and me.

The ring of fire was enlarged but it took over an hour to convince the ants that a detour was in order. By the time we had gotten rid of our uninvited guests, it was dawn and time to start hunting again.

This should answer any question about Africa's most dangerous game.!

CHAPTER 5
Put A Cobra In Your Car

The rain pattered the roof of the safari car as we drove along muddy roads west of Beira in Mozambique in 1960; this was before the terrorists took it away from the Portuguese. Our professional hunter, Giberto Barros, kept repeating his refrain, ''Zis iss ze dry season. It will stop.'' Not only did it not stop, it got worse. We camped in a makeshift thatched-roof building where the constant misty rain made me dream I was in a shower.

The day we started hunting the elusive nyala (Mozambique is famous for this striped bronze antelope with gracefully curved horns), the rain poured down, the road became invisible and we sloshed through shallow lakes of muddy water. Finally, we slowed to a stop in an impossible mudhole.

Giberto, conscious of his rank as boss, sat in the driver's seat shouting orders.

Frank and I got out of the car to help dig and push, but not Giberto. At last the rain let up and Frank suggested I take the cameras to keep them from being splattered with mud and walk ahead about 100 yards where we could see a conical termite hill rising above the waving grass. I could perch there and wait until they got the car out of the mud.

After a time, the car moved; I could see the men turn it around and I figured they would go back to the edge of the plain behind them and skirt the woods. So I shouldered the cameras and slogged onward to the other edge of the open meadow where mopane trees rose in a jumbled forest.

When the men picked me up, they had a hair-raising story

to tell. As we drive on our many safaris, I am usually the one who sits up front in the middle, straddling the gears. Frank is on the outside ready to jump out for a quick shot. The gun bearers and helpers ride in back. Through the years, I have become expert at draping my legs around the gears.

Now, as the men were slowly driving past a low bush, the branches swept the side of the car and a huge cobra, resting on a branch to keep out of the water, dropped into the front seat of the car and landed exactly where I should have been sitting.

Before Giberto realized what had happened, the cobra slid over his lap and stuck its head up through the spokes of the steering wheel. There it was, staring him right in the face.

Giberto shrieked, ripped open the car door and fell clumsily into the swamp. Frank made the same maneuver on his side of the car after getting over his first shock.

The safari car, in low gear, slogged along with no occupants except the cobra curved upright in the driver's seat as if it were driving the vehicle.

Presently the car smashed into a bush and stalled. Then the question was how to get the cobra out of there. The Portuguese are volatile and the natives imitate them, so that pandemonium was ensured. The cobra reacted accordingly, — swished at by branches in the hands of the natives, it hid under the seat where it was finally able to make an exit out of reach of the flailing leaves.

All of which impels me to say: If I had not left the car to protect the cameras from flying mud, I would have had a flying cobra in my lap.

II: AN ELEPHANT TOO CLOSE FOR COMFORT

One day, in Botswana several years later, we were on safari looking for a big elephant or greater kudu. Frank and Andrew Holmberg, our professional hunter on many other trips in Kenya, parked the car under a huge wild fig tree that provided dense shade from the sun. The men and the gun bearer, an old friend of other safaris called Sungura, trudged down a grassy path to a waterhole. Once in the blind, they could watch the animals come to drink and hope that a huge bull might come along. I was left in the safari car with the driver.

It was getting hot even in the shade, so I wrestled a cushion from the Land Rover and grabbed a book to read until the men came back. I walked a few yards away to a shady tree and lay down to read, my binoculars beside me in case I might see a new kind of bird. Bees hummed all around adding to my drowsiness. Soon I was asleep.

Whoosh, wheeoo, whoosh! startled me awake.

Opening my eyes, I stared up into the face of an enormous bull elephant. Apparently the car and I were well hidden and no errant breath of air had warned the bull, for there he was looking down at me.

His eyes fairly bulged as he gazed but so did mine. I suppose, as usual, it was only a few seconds, but it seemed like minutes. The big bull's beautiful head with ears standing out on either side like enormous wings, were set against a blue, blue sky. What a picture he would make! Why on earth hadn't I grabbed my camera when I got out of the car?

The bull was just as surprised as I was and not in the least belligerent, so I moved very slowly on all fours, crawling to the car in the hope of getting the picture of a lifetime. But the panorama was shattered by a scrambling noise from the direction of the car.

The driver was hysterically trying to climb the fig tree from the roof of the car. This ruined the whole set up.

My big friendly bull turned to look at the driver, then back at me where I was crawling by inches toward the car. Majestically he turned around and ambled away from us down the path to the waterhole as if nothing had happened.

When the men returned, they were laughing. It seems that Sungura had climbed a tree in order to see what animals were approaching the waterhole so as to warn the men of their coming. He saw the elephant come up and knew I was under a tree there. He began to jump up and down in the tree calling to the men, "Memsahib, Memsahib, big elephant will step on her."

The men were amused but not too concerned about my

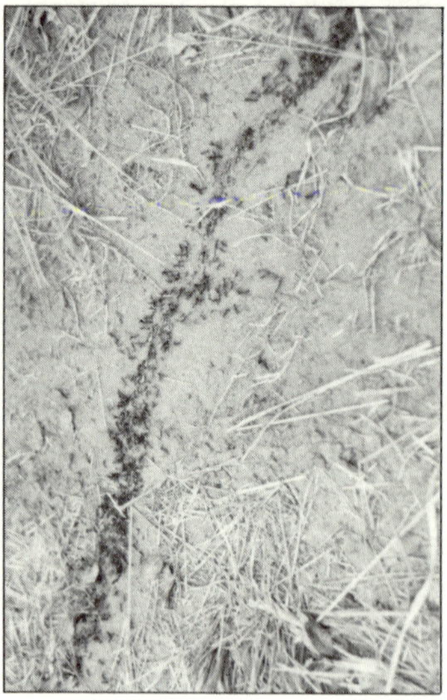

Above: Bull elephant is contemplating making a false charge to remove us and to teach us to mind our own business.

Left: Safari ants on the march.

Left: Rough going on safari — Mozambique.

Below: The popular stance of the Dinkas is to rest on their spears and give the appearance of storks.

safety — I come last in consideration on a safari, the animals come first. So they just let nature take its course. But my affection for Sungura deepened; he was the only one who wanted to protect me, which reminds me of another anecdote in another region entirely. I call it —

III. THE CASE OF THE INNOCENT BYSTANDERS, OR DON'T MESS WITH MOOSE

Several years ago in the 1940s on our way to a hunt in northern Canada in the middle of September, we drove by way of Yellowstone Park, hoping that the tourists might have gone home for the winter. We hoped to get some good movies of animals and birds undisturbed by mobs of people.

Driving along the road which paralleled the Yellowstone River, we noticed a large bull moose contemplating the river. He obviously wanted to cross over to our side. Frank immediately decided to take up our movie camera and tripod and try to get a shot of the moose swimming. Noting that the large meadow between us and the river contained nary a tree or bush to hide behind, and remembering several hair-raising adventures we had already had with bull moose, I hesitated. Wouldn't we be sitting ducks if the moose took offense?

Frank, of course, was not to be deterred, so with a sigh, I opened the car door and followed him with the still camera. Perhaps the presence of two people instead of one would keep the moose from charging. And if Frank were to be trampled, I wanted to be there beside him.

As we stumbled along, crouching, the moose made up his mind and slowly entered the water. Frank was as near as even he thought advisable, and set up the tripod while I crouched behind him.

I am sure that animals vary in their facial expressions as much as people; that moose had an ugly disagreeable face. I looked behind me. There was not a stick to hide behind. The pine forest, bordered by willows, was 500 yards away. On the banks of the river 100 yards from the trees were two fishermen. That was all.

I turned back and watched as the moose came out of the water and shook himself. He eyed Frank with distaste.

"I don't like his looks. You'd better go back and head for those fishermen. There is safety in numbers and this moose looks mean."

What an understatement. The moose stamped and snorted agreement with Frank.

"I won't go without you," I murmured, unconvinced.

"I'm coming," replied Frank. "I can always catch up with you. Hurry!"

I started back and heard the thud of Frank's feet right behind me. My own feet felt as if leaden weights were attached to them. It was like a slow motion dream. I put every ounce of strength into running but I seemed to be standing still. It was a real nightmare.

"Shift into high, he's gaining on us," shouted Frank, beside me now.

"I can't go any faster," I sobbed out of breath.

By now, the fishermen were aware of us — two running figures heading for them with an enraged moose snorting close behind. They dropped their rods and began to run for the trees. The moose gained on all four of us.

Then we spied a huge open culvert ahead of us. Large enough to crawl into, it was a heaven-sent refuge! Frank called to the fishermen to head for it and we followed suit and barely made it.

As I crawled in, the moose let out a great snort of frustration. Then, after a few minutes of stamping around, he quit and headed back to the river.

"Well," said Frank, "I've always heard there was safety in numbers, but that moose hadn't heard of it."

The fishermen cast disgusted looks at us for bringing them into this mess, didn't even inquire who we were and returned disconsolately to their interrupted fishing.

CHAPTER 6
Dinkas In the Sudan

''He does look like a stork, doesn't he.'' I said to Frank who had described the Dinkas before we arrived in their part of the Sudan — the well-known Sudd — or vast swamps of the Nile just north of Uganda.

Ahead of us a group of ebony warriors stood watching our approach in an antique rented Chevrolet ''box car'' or van. They stood on one leg leaning on their spears, statuesque, six to seven feet tall, naked except for assorted beads strategically placed around their waists.

The Dinkas were utterly unselfconscious with their beautiful bodies and noble bearing. Intelligent, proud faces, noses slightly aquiline and a twinkle in their eyes, a ready smile, they surrounded us with genuine friendliness.

We stopped the car and asked, by use of sign language, if we could take their pictures. They responded by posing stiff as daguerreotypes.

We knew we were probably the first foreigners in these parts in many years. We had been trying to get into the southern Sudan since 1956, but the Arabs in the north were fighting with the blacks in the south and there was no tourist travel until the country settled down.

Now it was 1959, five years since the English pulled out.

We had permission to do excavating where the Blue and White Nile come together near Khartoum after which we flew to Juba in the south where a Greek fixed us up with an impromptu safari consisting of a cook who spoke a little English, a reckless driver and a game guide. Our equipment was as meager as our food.

Attracting the Dinkas' attention away from our cameras was almost impossible. One of the warriors stood out resplendently in a girdle of many-colored bead strings which formed a corselette around his middle. Since he was otherwise unadorned, the effect of this decoration was startling.

We had flown to the Sudan in luxurious comfort. We approached Khartoum and the sinuous Nile had shimmered in the heat even though it was only February. Nightgowned red-sashed Arabs potted around the airport in bare feet. We had looked forward to a few days at a famous hotel on the banks of the Nile — spacious gardens and modern facilities — and we had made reservations weeks early to ensure our reception. However, when the clerk handed our room key to a boy who led us out the front door, we knew we were headed for the old battered Nile steamer which was anchored in front of the hotel and was used for overflow guests. It turned out that the Red Chinese were the favored ones this time and they had "taken over" the entire hotel. Thus, the English and Americans were ostracized to the boat and even with the help of the American ambassador, we were unable to obtain a decent room. We looked on as Russians, Czechs and Chinese swaggered about demanding the best of everything and getting it.

That evening, our dismay was crowned by the sight of rats running to and fro on the ropes that tied us to the shore.

The red tape took many days to unwind, first to get our camping clothes out of bond, which took the combined efforts of Scandinavian Airlines and our embassy and then to get permits to carry guns and hunt, permits to carry cameras, more permits to use the cameras, ad infinitum.

We learned that Equatoria was a closed restive area because the blacks hated their new Arab masters in the northern part of the Sudan and because the slave trade was still active, especially on the borders of Ethiopia.

At long last we enplaned for Juba, relaxing in the knowledge that our pilot was an Englishman of long experience. Flying over the desert with its heat waves is always rough and native people often get air sick. So we were happy to emerge into fresh air — even though hot — and to be met by an elderly Greek friend who awaited us.

We drove to the Juba Hotel, a rustic affair in a mass of white flowering frangi-pani bushes. Our room was a small dome-topped cottage with revolving fan in the the dome, which urged the hot air up and hopefully out. The hotel must have been charming when the English were in Juba; now it was very much run down, the swimming pool a stagnant mosquito pond, the tennis court useless, the dusty roads pitted and rough. Black kites circled above us — the indispensable refuse workers of Egypt and the Sudan.

Our Greek friend, Mr. Yiamanis, drove up the next day to see us begin our three-week jaunt. He supplied us with the ancient Chevrolet box car, our crew, food, cots and bedding.

Our driver, Kamoun, was a cocky black who spoke no English and was inclined to speed up when any giggling native girls were in sight. He had complete disregard for cars, chickens, goats, children or anything in his way.

Kisanga, our cook, was the only one who spoke English. Trained by the English, he did very well with our meager supplies. Rihani, our official game scout, was persistent but inexperienced.

Our first night in the rest house at Amadi was delightful. A day bumping along those incredibly dusty roads and through monotonous scenery of sparse deciduous woods, with walking natives always in sight, gave us no feel of wild Africa. The birds, however, were unbelievable. Melodious songs filled the air. The call of the "pumper bird" was incessant (they were tiny barbets), and reminded us of India. I was thrilled by the flashing greens and reds of the bee eaters, the brilliant blue flashing of wings of the rollers and especially the huge loury or turaco — an iridescent dark green with a white-crested head setting off red-rimmed eyes, and a bright red underside to their wings that appeared to burn as they flew.

Everywhere, we could see the imprint of the English — well laid-out roads, park-like villages, houses surrounded by gardens, teak plantations with enormous crackly dead leaves underfoot, even a small garrison at Amadi with soldiers who marched out to lower the flag and sound taps at dusk. But everything was untidy and down at the heels. The people were trying to carry on but without know-how and the real ability. However, the frangi-pani bushes, the brilliant bougainvilleas and many other exotic plants punctuated the extensive green lawns and young people played soccer in the cool of the evening and there was no denying the atmosphere of the place.

At Yirol, we stopped to check in with the police — this was required at every town in Equatoria, the new name for the southern Sudan — and were arrested. The local official read our permits.

We somehow lost. confidence as we saw him hold our papers upside down while he pretended to read them. As far as he was concerned, we were foreigners and he had been told to arrest foreigners.

Our uneasiness magnified when a long line of prisoners with balls and chains was marched by. Political prisoners, we were told. Fortunately, the district commissioner happened to come by at this moment and, seeing our predicament, released us. We still wonder what might have happened if he hadn't intervened when he did.

So now we were surrounded by our first Dinkas. Tall and well built, some shiny with grease, some powdered with light gray ashes to ward off insects, others with bead corselettes or with nothing but an ostrich feather stuck in their hair. Women with lively expressions, a cape or piece of cotton wrapped around them, came up close to see if we were real. I was probably the first woman in pants they had ever seen. While we were trying to take in every detail, they were doing the same.

They started to laugh when they saw my painted fingernails and lips; their long fingers examined me completely and all the while their laughter and carrying-on grew more deafening. When everyone was urged to join the fun, Frank and I left town hastily.

We drove for several hours approaching the flat open toich country of Lake Nyubor. When the Nile floods each year, the water gradually disappears, leaving a vast level plain covered with a lush growth of grass that attracts animals far and wide. This is called *toich*, home of the Dinkas who herd cattle and fish. The rare Nile lechwe lives here all year round in the vast swamps which remain wet even during the dry season. The lechwe (known as Mrs. Gray in memory of a famous English woman), is a water-dwelling antelope found only in this part of the Sudan and nowhere else.

The Dinkas were burning off the long grass to encourage short lush green grass for cattle feed. So as we approached the lake, the darkening sky was glowing with grass fires and fireflies.

It was long after dark when we drove up to the rectangular thatched rest house, only to find that the Dinkas had moved in. My heart sank. It's okay to watch tall naked people from a distance, but to be surrounded by them in the dark so that their odor suffocated us — this was more than I could stand at the end of an exhausting day.

"Don't tell me we've got to sleep with them too," I grumbled to Frank.

"Guess we'll have to be good sports." he said.

"Not on your life. You've gone too far this time. I'll sleep in the car or out in the grass with the mosquitoes, but not with the Dinkas. Anyhow, I've decided I don't like them. They smell too bad."

The boys were busy unpacking our duffle as we stood in the dark trying to keep a little apart from the odor. Already we could see our mess boy moving Dinkas out of half the house and sweeping the dirt floor with a bunch of grass. Clouds of dust swirled up, the stench was appalling.

My spirits sank even lower.

"Frank, I've just got to go to the bushes and there aren't any. You have to go with me in the dark out there." I could hear pig-like grunts of hippos wallowing and a peculiar snapping sound which we learned later were land snails, used by Dinkas as toys for their children. They are also carriers of the dread disease called bilhartzia, which can attack the liver of people who live along the Nile.

"Okay, come on," Frank said in disgust. Not seeing in the dark as well as he could, I held his hand and proceeded into the unknown. Only the glowing horizon of distant grass fires and occasional fireflies lighted our way. Suddenly my left foot sank into a bottomless pit, I skinned my shin as I fell and it left me sitting on the ground with one leg wrenched and suspended in the hole. I burst into tears.

"This is the last straw," I moaned. "Now all I need is more dysentery from their old flies." (This unwanted wish was later fulfilled.)

Frank began to chuckle. "You would have to fall into a Dinka outhouse!" he said comfortingly.

Back at the rest house, we found Kisanga had made our half-house almost livable except for the smell. But the white-washed mud walls rose only six feet high so that the Dinkas in the other half of the house were clearly audible. However, our cots were up with mosquito nets, a table was set with cloth, and Kisanga was brewing tea. My sense of humor was still at low ebb in spite of hot soup and canned meat, but those cots looked clean and inviting.

In the middle of the night we were awakened by moans. Light flickering on the thatched roof showed that our Dinka neighbors had built up their fire to heat water. The moans increased, punctuated by coughing and wheezing.

"Is someone having a baby?" asked Frank, sleepily recalling all those movies where people endlessly boil water for this blessed event.

We lay there listening, longing for sleep. but it was out of the question so we just lay there on our backs watching the firelight flickering on the thatch above us.

"Can't be rain," Frank suddenly remarked.

"Don't be silly," I retorted.

"Well, something is spattering my face."

"I don't feel anything. It's your imagination or else those mosquitoes —" I looked up. Far overhead hung a colony of huge bats and Frank's head was directly beneath them.

"You deserve it for laughing at me when I fell in that hole."

In the morning light after a few fitful hours of sleep, our discomfort seemed endurable. The crowding Dinkas didn't seem to smell quite so bad in the daylight and their friendly smiles and offers to help pack us up dispelled my antagonism. Several were gray with a coating of cow dung plastered to their bodies with fish oil. We never did learn if it was for mosquito protection or just decoration.

We both looked forward to our secluded camp which we set up several miles distant under a tamarind tree. We still weren't free of the Dinkas — even here they appeared out of nowhere. But they were always eager to help and never stopped giggling at our odd ways.

The next day Frank went hunting the Nile lechwe with two seven-foot Dinkas. Since Frank couldn't pronounce their names, he called one "Hey You" and the other "You There." The Dinkas seemed to think this a compliment and learned to answer to these names.

Frank was going to wade waist deep in the swamp all day and I declined, shouldering my movie camera on the chance I might encounter something unusual on the path between arms of the swamp.

I watched egrets, storks and other water birds and the morning proved fascinating. Then, suddenly about a hundred yards ahead of me, appeared two warriors with spears aimed at my middle. They started running straight at me.

My heart sank. What had I done to deserve this end? My knees barely held me upright.

No one ever told us Dinkas were dangerous; just as I was about to cave in, they stopped ten feet from me, raised their spears upright and stuck their points into the ground and crumpled with laughter — this was their idea of a joke.

Afterward, they took my camera and carried it back to camp for me. However, it was some time before I got over the shock of their charge — my own personal moment of truth.

When Frank returned with his lechwe for the museum, he related that the same thing had happened to him as well as another joke they played.

The Dinkas knew where every deep hippo pool lay in the path they were following. So as they sloshed along, without warning he sank into one of the holes, holding his rifle above his head, but otherwise totally immersed. When he came up blubbering, the Dinkas were bent over laughing.

In all of this — with ups and downs, jokes and frights and horrible smells, the Dinkas became our friends. Their way of life was perfect for them and they were such a happy, self-sufficient people.

When the civilized world engulfs their small piece of paradise, what will happen to the proud, tall bearers of spears with their quick flashing smiles and their ready sense of humor?

Top Left: Frank rests on safari in Africa.
Top Right: Brownie and my Grants gazelle.
Bottom: Cheetah and dead wildebeest.

CHAPTER 7
Tiger Trouble

"He is only an ordinary tiger," explained Rao Naidu. "You have come to India from your country to find a really big tiger — a real man eater. You can't be bothered with this local tiger."

Frank rose from his seat on the veranda. "We have never even seen a wild tiger. The ones at home in the Albuquerque zoo are all tame and enjoy having their necks scratched, they purr like sewing machines. Let's go and see this tiger anyway."

Meanwhile, a Hindu with a green dhoti wrapped around him like a diaper was prostrating himself to Rao, begging for help. Palms together, the custom in greeting, he was bowing and begging. But Rao continued shaking his head.

"What is he saying?" Frank asked.

"He is saying there is a tiger down the road growling at everyone who walks past. The people want you to come and kill it."

Since Hindus have no guns and are (religiously speaking) at the mercy of tigers, leopards and cobras, we could well understand the man's predicament.

Frank's eyes lit up with excitement. "Gosh," he said, "a tiger is a tiger is a tiger in my league. Let's go take a look." He was already in the hallway grabbing his gun and I was hanging cameras on my shoulder.

But Rao protested. "No one bothers with a tiger that has killed less than a hundred people."

His words fell on deaf ears. Frank was already nearly out of hearing range. Assorted helpers rushed to catch up with us. A sahib or memsahib never carries anything in India. There are always more helpers than anyone needs for menial tasks. So Rao was hard put to catch up with Frank; I was breathlessly trying to keep up myself.

Frank and I had gone to Greece in 1956 on a Ford Foundation grant to finish research on a book he was writing on prehistoric man in Europe. Most of our time had been spent in Greece, Asia Minor, Egypt, Iraq and Iran, but being so near India, Frank stretched our interests to include a famous site in Pakistan, Mohenjo Daro, and on to India.

So what could be more logical than to spend two weeks tiger hunting? This was 1956 when there were still plenty of tigers and not quite so many people.

Frank contacted a shikar firm and arranged a tiger hunt with Rao Naidu, one of the foremost hunters in Madhya Pradesh. So here we were after a more or less comfortable train trip followed by an interminable dusty road and a very slow drive among myriads of bullock carts and people who paid no attention to our horn. We arrived at the rest house — a relic of the days when the English managed the teak forests and bamboo groves — and at last we found ourselves in relative comfort.

The beds of woven ropes were comfortable allowing air to circulate underneath. The heat was ghastly. The house, by the village of Arjuni, was white with a red roof, built on top of a knoll to catch the breeze. The bare trees reminded us of Pennsylvania in winter; the ground, however, was littered with enormous crackling teak leaves. Where was the jungle we had heard so much about in Kipling?

The toilet really amused us. It was complete with a mahogany seat ensconced on top of several steps like a throne. The usual potty helper, however, proved a bit too industrious and one day tried to remove the pot while it was being used.

Rao had hired eleven servants to wait on us. There was the cook, the cook's helper (so he wouldn't have to exert himself by having to look for something he needed), a helper to help the helper, a waiter, a waiter's helper, and so on. The shoeshine boy removed our shoes constantly to wipe off the dust whenever we returned to the house and sat down on the porch.

Starting out before dawn the day after we arrived, we were startled by luminous eyes reflecting in the head lights of the Jeep. A flutter of wings — which we realized didn't belong to the bushbabies of Africa who also have huge catlike nocturnal eyes — but to night jars or night hawks with bright white wing bars. They had spent the night dusting themselves in the road.

Occasionally as we drove, a chital dashed across the road, its pretty spotted body gracefully flashing out of sight. A shadow at the side of the road was a huge gaur — a water-buffalo-sized animal with blue eyes, very shy. Startled peacocks flew ahead with their long tails waving behind them.

Once in a while Rao stopped the Jeep to look at tracks in the road, hoping to find the huge tiger we were hunting. I got out to look and was amazed that there were no mouse or rat tracks or any other signs of small life.

"What on earth do leopards and tigers eat?" I asked Rao.

"The cattle and buffalo of the natives are now their main diet, I am afraid," answered Rao.

"Well, there are plenty of them," I said, "and it looks as if there are plenty of people to spare now."

As daylight lightened the forest, we turned off the headlights and began to see and hear the birds.

The mournful cooing of doves took us back to Africa where there are various kinds everywhere. Mynah birds chattered, flocks of noisy beautiful parrots darted by, their underwings a contrast of yellow to their iridescent green bodies. Perching among the orange flowers of the palas trees, the parrots made a lovely picture. We heard a tiny barbet begin his "pumping" noise, a monotonous unmusical "pump, pump, pump" never stopping to take a breath. Returning to the village, two kinds of huge crows cawed bitterly over the absence of a stray tidbit.

This, the universal cry of India, hunger.

As we returned in late morning for our breakfast, the people had started to lead their buffaloes, bullocks and assorted mongrel dogs and children to the tiny pond which was all that was left of the river in the dry season. Rao informed us there was a timetable for the use of the dwindling water. Leopards, tigers and other large animals took over the pond at night. In daylight people took over and again in late afternoon.

We watched the procedure with horror. Small boys climbed onto the backs of buffaloes to scrub the dust which was thick in every crack of their skin. The women washed clothes, bathed themselves and drank — all in the same water.

''What happens if the tigers drink late or the people come early?'' I asked.

''That is just too bad,'' replied Rao with a wry grin.

''Why do the men carry those silly little axes over their shoulders on the road and why do all the women carry umbrellas?'' I asked another question.

''That is to keep the tigers from jumping on them,'' Rao answered. ''A tiger usually follows his prey and then jumps for the neck. That is, if he is an orthodox tiger. If something is sticking up, he hesitates or retires.''

Startled, I began to think of myself. If I took a walk, the camera wouldn't help. Oh yes, the tripod! I was relieved.

Resting in the middle of the day, luxuriantly sipping iced orange juice and getting used to the efficient service, we watched the bullock carts lumber by with their loads of swaying bamboo poles, teak logs and thatching grass. As we sat there, a boy came out and pulled off Frank's socks. He was going to wash them to try to earn his meager salary because as yet he had had nothing to do.

In the late afternoon, when a cool breeze sifted through the bare trees, we started out on patrol again, to look for tracks of the big tiger. Again, nothing.

A late and delicious dinner awaited us after we were forced to shower and change clothes as was the custom of the long-gone English. The dinner, too, was reminiscent of English customs — for we must have a fish course, by all means — even if it were sardines.

We finished dinner and could hardly wait to pile into bed. Suddenly drums began to beat, flutes tootled and there was a tin pan noise of cymbals beating against our ears. Rao informed us this was the marriage season and people were celebrating.

''How can we sleep with all this racket?'' mumbled Frank.

"You will get used to it," said Rao. "We can't stop it."

That was that. Our sleep was troubled by fearful dreams of catastrophes, but we did manage to snooze between the blasts of crazy exuberance.

When we were roused for the morning hunt, we drowsily sipped our coffee, ate toast and tumbled into the Jeep, half conscious. Nothing happened, so we sat like zombies,the dust surrounding us flowing like water into the car ruts as we passed. We had such a liberal coating we wouldn't have been recognized by our best friend at home.

By the time we returned for breakfast, we were worn out. Sitting on the veranda thinking about collapsing onto our beds, we watched a native run up to us, two sticks in his hand.

He had seen the tracks of a large tiger.

Rao explained that one stick was the length of the track and the other its width. Rao thought it might be worth while to get a look, so he sent some men out to build a machan in a tree overlooking the farther end of the pond. The tiger would surely come to water and this was the only water for miles around. The men started off carrying one of the rope-plaited beds, assorted other ropes and a rope ladder.

At dusk when the men set out for the machan, I decided to walk out with them. I hated to miss any of the fun. There was room on the machan for three people: Frank, Rao and the man who held the powerful flashlight. Since there was now a steady procession of animals and people going to the pond and back, I felt perfectly safe and could saunter back to the house at my leisure, watching birds on the way. There were so many harmonious calls that I didn't know — so much to learn.

After saying goodbye to the men and good luck, I turned around. The house was still in sight in the distance and people were moving slowly along in both directions.

Suddenly I stopped. There, right on top of our own tracks, was the imprint of a large tiger paw. The animal had walked practically in our midst and no one had seen it. Impossible! But there it was. I looked furtively around — not one shrill peacock had warned a tiger was near, not one single langur monkey had chattered. But then, the main enemy of the langurs was the leopard. Perhaps they ignored tigers. Leopards climb trees to get monkeys, but tigers are ground animals.

My heart began to pound. Under their own volition, my feet began to move, and I found myself walking as fast as I could to rejoin the people. There was safety in numbers. But how could a brightly-striped tiger walk unnoticed in those open woods?

The next day was an imitation of the one before. We heard sambar deer belling and the strident call of the peacocks broke the stillness. The bright black eyes of the peacocks are the first to spy danger of any sort and they, with the chattering of the monkeys, are the policemen of the jungle.

That evening, I decided that it was a once-in-a-lifetime chance that a tiger would walk in the presence of so many people, so I joined the men again as they went to take up their vigil on the machan. Besides, I needed exercise. The continual Jeep riding bothered my back. Again, on my return to the house, there was a tiger track on top of ours. This was my last walk alone.

At noon the next day, we sat on the veranda, relaxing after the usual morning drive when a native ran up with the news of the growling tiger.

We started off with a bevy of helpers carrying guns, cameras and such. We had not gone more than a hundred yards up the road, still in sight of the house, when we heard a low growl to our right. We halted as if at a signal. We could see nothing. Open tree trunks with small clumps of bushes that couldn't hide a chicken.

"He must be in that bush," Frank said in a low voice. He advanced cautiously, but the huge dry teak leaves crackled under his feet and we heard another warning growl.

"That's no way to greet strangers," I whispered nervously. Another growl greeted my whisper.

"I think we go back," said Rao.

"I think we go back, too," muttered Frank.

Rao sent our helpers to the village to round up some twenty-five villagers for a beat to drive the tiger out into the open. A small group returned with the usual bed, rope and ladder to build a machan on the other side of the growl.

I watched the men. They would need no flashlight in the

daylight but how was I to climb up that snaky ladder being dreadfully afraid of swaying heights?

My answer came immediately. "You are to stay on the ground back where we first heard the tiger. If he comes in your direction, get some movies."

I swallowed that morsel of male chauvinism and replied, "Oh, I see. You climb a tree and sit there in safety while I pose as tiger bait."

"You can climb a tree," Frank said. I had never climbed a tree even in my childhood. "Besides, think of the swell movies you may get."

"Oh, yeah!"

The men clambered up the ladder and I retreated with two helpers to a position on the opposite side of the tiger from the machan. Looking up into the tree against which I was leaning, I wondered just how scared I would have to be to actually climb it, or whether it would be more expedient to slam the tiger on the nose with my camera and tripod if he attacked.

Soon came the sounds of men beating tin pans, shouting and blowing whistles. They appeared in a long line, pounding on tree trunks, beating the ground.

Suddenly a shot rang out. Another shot.

"What on earth is happening?" I muttered. Frank couldn't have missed at that short distance. I strained my eyes to try to see between the tree trunks. No striped form coming in my direction.

Then a rush of voices and I saw a cluster of beaters running in mad confusion. What happened? Should I join them and run too or, like the boy on the burning deck, stand and face it out?

I shouted to the passing natives to ask what was going on. None spoke English. I picked up my movie camera to use as a weapon if need be, and stood still, listening. Silence. No tiger. The men who had been protecting me disappeared. I decided to creep up the road in the direction of the machan and, on the way, I met one of the helpers coming back to fetch me.

Then I saw Frank, Rao and two other men leaning over something on the ground: a huge bronze-colored tiger.

"What happened?" I asked. "Why so many shots?"

"There were four tigers," Frank said, "— a mother and

Left: The "Dasas" very dark original population of India still hunt with bows and arrows. Very few are left.

Below: "Beaters" who flushed the tigers out of hiding, return to admire their tiger.

Opposite: Brownie and one of the two tigers shot by Frank. Mother was a man-eater teaching her young how to hunt.

three full grown cubs. I shot the mother as she came toward me when the beaters were nearly here. Then the three cubs dashed out and one of them almost caught one of the beaters as he shinnied up a tree. Rao told me to shoot the biggest one — a male. There he is over there."

I looked where he pointed and there was another striped beauty nearly as large as the mother.

After the picture-taking was over, the men loaded the two tigers on the hood and in the back of the Jeep and we started back. Frank and I had to walk because of the weight of the tigers on the Jeep: each one weighing somewhere between five and six hundred pounds.

As we neared the house, a mob of people rushed toward us, shouting and banging on drums. News had traveled fast. By the time we hiked up the slight hill to the house, we were completely surrounded, drums and flutes going full blast — the noise was frightful. After the tigers were unloaded, the men turned and carried Frank, much to his embarrassment, on their shoulders.

The crowd parted and two lovely young girls in graceful saris appeared carrying lighted lamps — dishes of coconut oil with wicks — and, approaching Frank they bowed low and kissed his feet.

Another coconut girl appeared and handed her dish to Frank who wondered what to do with it. Then she, too, bowed low and took some of the oil and poured it on his shoes.

Later after the people had gone, we relaxed on the veranda, admired the tigers hanging in a nearby tree and Rao explained the hunt to me.

The favorite food of tigers, he said, was wild boar. Our tigress had killed one and was sharing it with her three cubs. Although a tiger may be driven away from its prey in the daytime when the light bothers them, they will not leave a wild boar which is a real delicacy. Hence the growls which frightened villagers as well as me.

Also, Rao, explained, this tigress was a mankiller because, instead of the usual stripes, hers ended in beautiful rosettes and was, therefore, completely identifiable. Rao had asked Frank to kill the larger cub, for she had already been training them to kill people when food was scarce.

My uncharitable reaction to this bit of information was that there were certainly plenty of people to go around.

Today, there are even more people. Need I add, fewer tigers?

PART III

IN IRAN

CHAPTER 8
Iran

Were Alexander the Great to return to Iran today and to visit any of the isolated villages tucked here and there among the desert mountains, I doubt he would see any sweeping changes from the last 2,000 years.

Civilization is flying fast on the wings of airplanes and the waves of radio and television. Soon the cities of the world will lose their individuality. This is true to some extent in the cities of Iran. But paved roads have not yet penetrated into the sparsely settled villages; they go quietly on with their ancient customs.

As our plane flew over towering but denuded mountains separated by vast stretches of desert, the country itself seemed vaguely familiar to us. We had just come from India and the contrast was startling. There were no tree-covered mountains and few green valleys, but, on the whole, the vastness reminded us of New Mexico, our home.

The plane approached Teheran and we gasped at the beauty of the snow-covered Elburz Mountains which cut off the Caspian Sea from the rest of the country. Mt. Demavend rose over 18,000 feet as a backdrop to the east. It was more majestic than any mountain we had ever seen, perhaps with the exception of Mt. McKinley.

Our feelings of familiarity were dispelled on landing. Here were Iranian skull caps, longs robes and dark blue or black white-spotted chadors which covered the women, head and all. Here, too, were horses and wagons a la troika, reminiscent of Iran's northern neighbor, Russia.

The wide avenues were lined on either side by cemented ditches known as ''jubes,'' by which the pure mountain water cascades through the streets — pure when it enters Teheran, unspeakably filthy when it has gone only a few blocks.

Teheran as a whole has not yet attained a really cosmopolitan air. Small shops and desperately poor natives were and are sandwiched in between vast embassy buildings and palaces and although the gold domed mosques are an Arabian Nights dream, the poverty of the masses is appalling to a Westerner.

However, Frank and I had not come to Iran in 1957 to dwell in cities. We had come to study archaeology and to hunt. Soon we were speeding south to spend the night in a village. We learned that almost all the villages were owned by the wealthy men of Teheran. The ancient feudal system was still in effect. Although the Shah had divided many of the royal estates into small farms, few of the wealthy clique had been persuaded to follow suit. This meant that, after a year of hard labor, the average villager had to give from two- to three-fifths of everything to the owner, more of his harvest and livestock as taxes. In the end, he usually had less than two-fifths for himself and his family.

A few villages were owned by forward-thinking men who supplied tractors and other utilitarian equipment, but the need was vast and the country backward and the majority of villagers still used primitive farm implements and, overall, there was little change in food, customs or living conditions since ancient times.

We spent the first night in a village called Little Garden, some 100 miles south of Teheran, as guests of the owner and, as such, were ensconced in the guest room, a white-washed, immaculately clean place located in the headman's house. A recessed niche held a kerosene lamp, its stark simplicity reminding us of our Southwest Pueblo villages. But the wall-to-wall Persian carpet gave the room a warm glow. We took off our shoes on entering, as per custom, though our job was harder than theirs. We had to sit down to unlace our high hunting shoes while the Iranians just slipped off their slippers. After spreading our sleeping bags on the floor, we sat cross-legged (as long as our muscles could stand it) around a charcoal brazier.

This was an oriental brass affair with tray, set down on the rug in the middle of the room. Steaming tea was brought to us in a brass pot and poured into glasses the size of demitasse cups. A tiny dish of irregular lumps of sugar sat beside it. We learned to put a piece of sugar in our mouths and drink the tea through the sugar.

Meanwhile, we had had no glimpse of any women. True orientals, they were not allowed to be abroad when strange men were in sight. And contrary to American custom, only males could serve us.

We had been sent to this village by Prince Hossein Doblatshahi, son of the late Reza Shah. Since he could not join us for two days, he had supplied us with an old American command car and its Armenian driver and owner, Sarkís Ramsar. Sarkís spoke only German, so our conversation was somewhat limited. Sarkís was supposed to bring enough food to last two days, as the poor villagers could not be asked to supply anything. However, Sarkis had brought only eggs and tea, so we augmented with local pomegranates and delicious native bread somewhat similar to Indian bread in New Mexico and it was very adequate.

I never was able to get more than a glimpse of the chador-clad women in the kitchen who scrambled our eggs on a tiny hearth. This village, being far from the Caspian slopes where charcoal was processed, used a kind of tumbleweed which was skillfully reduced to coals. The weed was often brought in on camelback.

Evening came and we sat in the doorway and watched shepherds bring in flocks of sheep guarded by beautiful big broad-headed, densly-furred native dogs. Since Mohammedans consider dogs unclean as pigs, they never make pets of them nor do they even touch them unless they have to. But the dogs were well fed and seemed happy — unlike the half-starved canines of Egypt and Iraq.

Curiously, an Iranian dog has no ears or tail. These are removed as a protection against wolves. With no free appendage to hang onto, the wolves are at a disadvantage.

The sheep were penned inside dome-topped adobe

buildings for the night. A caravan of camels, carrying long canes that resembled wild rice, sauntered by. Since it was winter, the drivers wore heavy dark felt capes which served as winter coats, raincoats and occasionally sleeping bags.

Little Garden was not very hospitable to foreigners. I think I was the first foreign woman who had ever been there. Mossadegh had stirred up so much anti-western feeling in the years of his power that it still lingered in remote villages, especially near the sacred town of Qom. Needless to say, when we slipped into our bedrolls, turned out the lamp and I saw black heads in the window against the sky, apprehension kept me awake for some time. Those peering faces followed me into my dreams. Frank was restless, too, so I knew it was not my imagination.

Morning came and our fears of the night before receded. All that day we climbed bare rocky mountains for a glimpse of the wild red sheep. While gasping for breath on a promontory overlooking a vast expanse of desert, I saw an encampment of black tent Arabs, the famous nomads of Iran. Their black felt tents contrasted with the light sandy desert. I begged Sarkís to drive us near so I could get some pictures. He was horrified and would not even discuss it. He said we should always keep our distance from them, especially when in lonely parts of the country.

It wasn't too long after this or too far south, that two Americans were murdered by just such people and for no reason at all. Except that the Koran does give its blessing to those who kill an infidel.

Frank rejoined me on a high ridge where I crouched behind our movie camera hoping some unwary sheep would come my way. Frank explained that after a long difficult stalk, he had come within shooting range of some red sheep, but just as he was aiming, the sheep stampeded. He looked around to see what was wrong. Behind him his guides had put down their prayer rugs and had risen against the skyline to pray to Allah; their loud singsong chant made the sheep run even faster.

Our meager lunch of bread and cheese was augmented that day by the delicious pomegranates. Americans, we were told, are ignorant of the correct way to eat them. First they are massaged until their hard exterior becomes soft and spongy. This breaks the liquid capsules around each seed. Then a small hole is punctured at one end and the juice is sipped like orange juice. It is both thirst quenching and a convenient way to carry liquid in the desert.

That evening, instead of returning to Little Garden, Sarkís drove us up to an ancient caravanserai. It looked like the fort at Zinderneuf of Beau Geste fame. The spring outside the fortifications was roofed by an enormous adobe beehive-shaped dome. As we entered the huge wooden gates we came into a large courtyard, arranged so that camels could be unloaded onto a platform at camel height. The owners and guards of the caravans slept in rooms above the platforms that were reached by steep narrow stairs; the building was structured around an open courtyard where the goats and sheep were grouped by their owners. The entire affair used barrel vaulting and must have been very ancient.

We were led up one of the narrow twisting stairways to what apparently was a suite of two rooms, each with a small cooking hole in the middle of the floor, and with rounded archways overlooking the courtyard.

The odors which arose, to our dismay, from the assorted livestock and people, were anything but pleasant. Small windows opened outward so that an approaching enemy could be sighted from a distance. We found we could walk around the roof between the domes made by the barrel vaults.

There was a glorious desert sunset that evening and we went out to watch it only to find ourselves prisoners. The people in the other room whom we had never seen before had spread their carpets and were bowing to Allah, chanting their evening prayers at the tops of their lungs. I wondered if our nearness as infidels was the cause of the extra loudness. Before we retired in confusion, we received ill-boding glares from the worshippers. After that we stayed in our room until Sarkís rescued us.

There were two huge courtyards, we discovered, and in one of these was a small group of black tent Arabs with a few odoriferous goats and sheep. They did not seem to resent our company, but who knows?

In the dark the stars shone. The cold night wind fanned our cheeks and, as we snuggled deep into our sleeping bags, we felt at home. Somehow, wherever we get out and live close to nature, anywhere, we feel attuned to life.

The next morning we were up before dawn, sitting crouched and shivering in our little room while the Iranians finished their prayers. After a scanty breakfast of steaming tea, bread and eggs, we started our return trip to Little Garden where we were to meet Prince Doblatshahi and an American friend of his, Harry Schaab, who also enjoyed hunting.

Back at the village, the sun warmed the white-painted porch in front of our room and we were soon dozing. Frank went to the room to snooze and Sarkís slept in the car. I sat for a while admiring the vast desert flats and mountain ranges. Soon I heard a soft rustle. A woman appeared from around the corner and smiled. Then another and another, and soon I was surrounded by a group of giggling women with tiny children hanging onto their skirts peeking at me from their hiding places. (I was reminded in many ways of the Navajos in our Southwest — the ones who don't see tourists often.) They were dressed in dark woolen pants; some gathered at the ankles, others straight like ours. These were covered by colorful cotton dresses. On their heads were white, dish-towel-like scarves that came down around their necks instead of the long dark blue chadors.

Most of the women carried knitting of such complex patterns and basket weaves that I was amazed. Using sign language, they showed me their way and I showed them mine (I was knitting socks for Frank). With ohs and ahs and international exclamations, they examined my Navajo bracelets and felt the texture of my nylon jacket.

Then a cloud of dust on the roadway heralded the approach of the prince's Buick and my new-found friends scuttled away. In the process of packing up, I did get a few quick pictures of women and children, in doorways, hidden from the men. I was very careful as I had nearly precipitated an international incident in Iraq when a man resented my taking a picture of his wife.

After the open command car and its generous coating of dust, we sighed with relief as we rode in the comfort of the

Buick. It was now bitter cold. Off we drove to Qom where we had lunch at a passable hotel. The prince informed us that only a few years before, in the days of Mossadegh, this would not have been possible in the sacred city. Even now I was not allowed to get out of the car except at the hotel and when Frank and the prince went for a closer look at the courtyard of the spectacular gold and blue mosque (against a warning from the prince that it might be dangerous because of Frank's blue eyes) they hurried back with threatening crowds following them. I was huddled in the back of the car hoping no one would notice me. A few days afterward, we were informed that two Frenchmen were killed in the same place we had been and that no one even thought of punishing the murderers.

As we drove south out of the city by the dusty gravel road, I looked back at the adobe buildings and shining domes of the mosque. Now, years later, we hear that a huge oil field has been found there and that foreign interests will soon develop it.

The next village we stayed in was Amirabad, about two hours drive south of Qom at the foot of a snowy mountain range called (with good reason) Seventy Summits. This range of mountains bordered the flat plain and formed a jagged forbidding backdrop to the desert.

Here the men were to hunt sheep and ibex. We lived in comparative luxury — on the floor, of course, but the inevitable Persian rug was under us and it felt like home. The village was large and walled in, the one toilet facility deplorable — a deep hole in the ground, a brass pitcher and no door. No privacy. I wondered if I should hum a tune while occupying it.

Supper was a repast. Hossein had brought with him kettle upon kettle of rice, chicken, meat and cakes. A cloth was spread on the rug and we gorged ourselves on steaming rice, sizzling meat and hot tea.

The ibex hunt was organized and, early in the morning with the temperature near zero, we piled into the open command car. The men were on the hood, hanging on all sides like Keystone cops. We drove across country without losing anyone and stopped near the foot of the mountains. We were to hide in small blinds of piled rocks in a high pass between two precipitous peaks while some twenty natives drove the ibex and sheep past us. Since hunts of this kind had been perpetrated a long time before we arrived, we determined the ibex and sheep knew about it too. We saw one old monarch outlined against the sky watching us suspiciously.

The wind whistled through the pass with a cutting edge and I had to back up part of the way up the gully. I had my inevitable helper and from the look on his face I knew he was disgusted having to play nursemaid to a female. I set up the movie camera before my hands froze and carefully took a light reading, estimating distances to the places the animals might possibly cross, and then crouching with my neck as far down into my eider jacket as I could get it.

It was indeed a rugged and beautiful place: immense barren masses of rock rising ridge after ridge against the sky and extending as far as the eye could see. There was no vegetation at all except a few low bushes. How the animals survived was a mystery to me. My guide sat huddled in his heavy felt coat and skull cap and, since we could only communicate in sign language, there seemed no reason to carry on a conversation. Besides I was miserable and wondered why I had let myself in for this adventure. How on earth had I come to this remote, frigid mountain pass in Persia anyhow? I could have been home in the sunny Southwest minding my own business.

Just then shots rang out; I pulled my head out of my collar to look around. A tiny figure of a man was barely visible against the skyline. Nothing else moved.

I had just crouched again when I heard a rattle of rocks and looking down into the valley, I saw a band of ewes and lambs heading up the mountain.

What luck! They were headed my way exactly where I had positioned the camera. This rarely happens in nature photography. I eased myself into position and pressed the button. The sheep came on obligingly and trotted all the way to the crest above me. When they disappeared, I sank back and began swinging my arms, coal miner fashion, to get life back into them.

After that it got steadily colder. I decided the shoot was over and began to take down my camera. Signaling to my guide,

I started back down the gully. On the way, I came upon Sarkís who had shot a poor ewe as the band galloped past. Most of the natives of Asiatic countries, I notice, have no qualms at sex or size of any game as long as it is edible. Slowly the men assembled: Frank, Prince Hossein and Harry were all empty-handed. The big ones had slipped away.

Back at the village we huddled on our Persian rug warming our hands by the brass brazier of coals and sipping tea through sugar lumps. Later the bowl of steaming rice with chicken hidden in its depths revived our spirits. That night I could have used an extra eider sleeping bag.

And so the hunt went. I gave up the next day from cold, dysentery and exhaustion and started back to Teheran with Harry who was going back before Frank.

The next phase of our trip took us to Hamadan, a beautiful modern city with a fine hotel we had no time to enjoy — wide boulevards, stately mansions, rows of trees along the street, all backed by snowy mountains. We saw the usual adobe hovels on the outskirts but they were not so numerous here.

We drove to a village that one of our friends owned. The villagers expected us — how word got to them I will never know. Driving up, we noticed a group of men holding a sheep. As we approached, they cut off its head with one stroke of a long knife and rolled it in front of the car. A grisly greeting to say the least.

We drove on a few yards and stopped near an adobe house with a white-walled entranceway flanked by a peach orchard, pink blossoms unfolding and stretches of grass and gardens.

Edging the adobe wall were weeping willows with leaf-fringed boughs making a waterfall of green. A rose garden in front, flowing water in ditches and a pond — the kind of Persian garden made famous by Persia's ancient poets.

We wandered around for a time enjoying the beauty and peace of the place when suddenly a boy appeared with a large brass tray. On it were sizzling shishkabobs, yogurt and steaming tea. To eat such a meal in a lovely garden is an experience that remains fresh in my memories. Later on, we explored an ancient bath built partly underground by a king of old Mesopotamia and still used by the local people. At the edge of the village rose a tall mound or tell with the remains of ancient adobe walls, pottery and sling stones eroding from the sides. The villagers had dug corrals into its base for their sheep. On the roof of one thatched building was a stork.

After a few hours, we drove to another village where we were to spend the night. The adobe houses here were more prosperous: the gardens were all walled with orchards lush with grass and running water.

We spent the night in a guest house which had a second story overlooking the orchard — an artist's dream. Though the mountains were more distant here than at the other village, the water descended with such force that it was piped to the second story where it made a fountain on the open veranda. The same water ran under the floor to a toilet. A novel and successful operation, however, it lacked the privacy of a door.

The moon was full and standing on the balcony looking down on the garden and adobe houses, and on to the snowy mountains, I had my second Arabian Nights dream.

The next day we went hunting. Mounted on small Arab stallions, we rode to a valley between two mountain ranges. Wild red poppies and tulips warmed the barren gray rocky slopes. There was no animal drive this time, which we had come to distrust. The wild animals were accustomed to them and they knew what to expect — better than we did. I saw a large bear tearing across a slope in the distance; Frank shot a huge boar but we saw no sheep or ibex. Our friends were not serious hunters. They talked constantly, laughed, played cards and shunned physical effort. So we decided to call it all off and return to Teheran.

Before we left Iran, however, Frank did get in two marvelous hunts with Prince Abdorreza, the Shah's younger brother, a true sportsman and excellent shot. I was not permitted to go along because Abdorreza's wife, the Princess Para Sima, was in Italy and protocol required her to accompany me.

As for the hunt, Frank rode the Princess' horse which had not been ridden for some time. No one but royalty or the guests of royalty can ride royal horses. On an English saddle, Frank felt very unsure of himself; the horse prancing forward, sideways, every way but the right way. Finally, the Prince said he thought Frank was holding the reins too tightly.

"Hell, your highness," responded Frank in dire distress, "if I give the horse more rein, we won't even be in the hunt."

Shortly after that, the shikars mumbled something to the Prince. Frank asked what it was and the Prince tactfully said that no one is allowed to precede royalty; Frank was, at the moment, ahead of the Prince. Again Frank struggled with the horse and was able to restrain him so that he held back just behind the Prince.

Every time they came to a gully, Frank's heart sank for he knew by that time that the horse would jump it, whether he reined in or not.

Years later we met the Prince and Princess at a banquet in Los Angeles and, seeing Frank, the Prince smiled broadly. He was soon recalling Frank's struggle with the horse. The Princess told me that the animal proved too much even for her and she had replaced it.

Before the hunt, the Prince had offered Frank his choice of guns. The array, mounted in gold and silver, were the gifts of various royalty who had hunted there. Frank carefully chose the least ostentatious, a gun which, during the hunt, fell apart when he pulled the trigger. The chagrined Prince gave him his own gun to use — and with which Frank bagged a fine ibex and a sheep, so the hunt was a success.

The picnic lunch afterward was one to remember: a table cloth spread out with much ceremony by the shikars, caviar and other delicacies — making our sandwich-picnics back home seem very inauspicious.

In 1966, we arranged a hunt with Tari Farmanfarmian, a cousin of the Shah who had been helping Prince Abdorreza establish game refuges to preserve the fast disappearing ibex, sheep, moufflon and even the possibly-still-extant Caspian tiger.

We toured the country via the tourist route and loved every minute of it. Then we headed north with Tari to hunt in the Elburz Mountains and visit the Caspian Sea. The barren mountains reminded us again of New Mexico in the southern desert regions of the state. The Caspian Sea was a disappointment to me because it was lukewarm and not very salty — just

Above: Iran - fortress of Bistram - remarkably well preserved after destruction by Genghis Khan centuries ago.

Opposite Below: Caravanserai from another angle.

Left: Iran - the caravanserai where we slept with the camel caravans.

not very exhilarating. But it was a good home to the sturgeon which, to the Russians' dismay, preferred to lay caviar eggs on the Iranian side instead of the Russian.

Again, Tari proved a perfect hunter and companion.

We visited the famous golden mosques in Isfahan, the unequalled silver workers and rug makers. We were especially interested in inlaid boxes made by tying bundles of triangularly cut and dyed camel leg bones and brass rods and glued to wood. There were examples of furniture made entirely in this manner.

In Shiraz, the gem of the poets, where Americans had established a modern hospital backed by the Mayo Clinic, and in nearby Persepolis, the ancient capital of the Persian dynasty captured by Alexander the Great, we saw the famous columns still upright as well as some with animal-carved heads lying on the ground. There were bas reliefs of ancient wars with soldiers marching up the impressive stairways. This, to me, was the prize archaeological site of all. The rocktombs of Darius and Xerxes were cut out of sheer rock walls nearby.

Both trips to Iran showed us, in equal measure, the good and the bad, the old and the new, the squalor of modernism beside the irretrievable treasures of the past. However, even though the Shah made many evident mistakes, he did try, not unsuccessfully, to bring his country to the modern world without destroying its ancient glory.

PART IV

IN OUTER MONGOLIA

CHAPTER 9
Outer Mongolia

I lay on a Russian-made cot in a Mongolian yurt and sleepily looked up at the domed ceiling in the center of which was a half circle of bright blue sky. Fanning out from this opening framed by a wooden ring was a wagon wheel, brightly painted wooden ribs with soft apricot and turquoise floral designs. The ribs reminded me of an open umbrella. The sides of the yurt were reinforced with wooden latticework. Over the spokes and latticework was an inch-thick layer of felt and canvas. Essentially unchanged, this was the kind of yurt used by Genghis Khan. In hundreds of years only the covering, canvas replacing the skins of former years, had changed.

In the center of the yurt was an ancient iron stove, its chimney poking through half the central vent. Beside it was a low table and around the edge of the yurt were four beds and two wardrobes — concessions to the modern world of newly-accepted tourists.

Outside, the early fall wind moaned around the flap which half-closed the opening in the yurt roof. Although the temperature was near freezing, Frank and I were snug.

I still couldn't believe we were in the middle of the Gobi Desert in Outer Mongolia. When I was young, I had heard Roy Chapman Andrews tell of his adventures exploring the Gobi Desert of China and Mongolia. He described it in the 1920s as a never-never land, where he discovered his famous dinosaur eggs. Nothing had changed in 1966 as far as we could see. It was easy to imagine myriads of horsemen spewing forth to conquer Asia and even a part of Europe. Civilization had only grazed this isolated country of friendly, fun-loving people during our visit in 1966 although we hear now that more tourists are going there than ever before.

How we got there is another story.

Frank often told me he wanted to go to Irkutsk in Siberia and from there to Lake Baikal and Outer Mongolia to continue his search for early man and to shoot the famous Argali sheep, the largest sheep in the world.

My heart quailed at the thought.

I was frightened to think of being so far from civilization in a Communist country and a place where our government couldn't possible extricate us if we got into trouble. One moment I fought the idea, the next I remembered the tales of Genghis Khan, Kublai Khan and Marco Polo. Deep down I wanted to see the Flaming Cliffs where Dr. Andrews had discovered the dinosaur eggs back in the 20s; I wanted to look into the eyes of the descendants of the Mongols who invaded and conquered Europe and who, now, were going to join the United Nations and belong to the modern world. In the end, my love of adventure won out.

After much maneuvering, we finally got permission to fly through Russia to Irkutsk in Siberia and from there to hunt the largest mountain sheep in the world — the Argali — in the Altai Mountains close to the Chinese border. But we were yet to encounter the devious channels of Russian bureaucracy.

First, we wanted to stop in Moscow for a few days. No, we were not allowed to stop. Then we wanted to fly to Tashkent and thence to Irkutsk — the shortest route from Iran where we would be hunting before going to Mongolia. Nyet on that, too.

In the end, we flew from Teheran to Moscow and transferred to a shabby jet (so noisy we had to stuff our ears with cotton) that took us to Irkutsk. All of this took a day and a night, so when we arrived in Irkutsk in the pouring rain, we were ready to fall thankfully into bed at the modern hotel where Intourist put us.

However, in 1966, modern in Russia meant no comfortable lobby to lounge in, inadequate heat when it was cold, sporadic water supply, floors with holes worn in them (even if recently laid) and door handles that come off in your hand.

In Irkutsk we were in the famed region of the Siberian taiga — endless rolling country heavily forested with beautiful white birch trees, pines and larch. Here we were welcomed by Russian archaeologists at a fine museum. And we spent a fascinating day at Lake Baikal, the deepest fresh water lake in the world, and the one with the greatest volume of water.

It grows deeper every year due to almost constant earthquakes. We were especially interested as it is the same type of earthquake fault that continues from the Middle East through Africa known as the Rift Valley.

With no warning, we were told to be at the airport in half an hour. At the time we didn't even have our visas for Mongolia although we had applied months before. However, this is the way things were done in Russia. At the airport we found ourselves surrounded by colorful Mongolians scrambling up the swaying ladder of an Ilyushin 14 — an old clunker similar to our old workhorse plane, the DC 3.

Our companions were nearly all Mongolians, dressed in the famous *del*, men and women alike. This is a Chinese-like garment unchanged through the centuries, high collar and loose sleeves, held in at the waist with a sash of contrasting color. The women were more apt to wear bright blue brocades and the men wore the more utilitarian and less expensive quilted kind. We were told that the only difference between winter and summer clothes was the number of layers underneath. For headgear, the men wore various types from ancient odd-shaped satin affairs to mens' felt hats and even berets. Most women had abandoned long braids and adopted the beehive hairdo over which they wrapped scarves and tied them in back rather than the peasant way of tying them under the chin.

No one we met then or later spoke English and we had to rely on our guide and interpreter, Surén, for all our information, while we desperately tried to sort out truth from fiction.

In Ulan Bator, an interview with Frank and me was broadcast at a once-a-week English program. The Mongolians were anxious for American dollars to help them catch up to modern times and we felt every effort was being made to teach English as a foothold in the modern world. Surén spoke excellent

English with only a few wrong words and he told us that he had learned from a victrola record.

When we approached the capital of Outer Mongolia, Ulan Bator, there were still patches of woods on the hillsides. A meandering river, the Tula, flowed through a beautiful valley. We disembarked and were held up for immigration and we had to admit we were uneasy. To be completely surrounded by Mongolians in their native *dels* made us wonder if, at heart, they were still the warlike cohorts of Genghis Khan. However, Surén did all in his power to make us feel welcome. As we drove into town he pointed out the vast encampments of yurts. These were to be abolished soon and in their places severe white concrete apartment houses built. We were not to photograph the yurts lest the world get the impression that Mongolians were backward people.

We passed through an enormous public square similar to Red Square in Moscow where we saw massive concrete buildings — government, opera, musuem and so on, with a statue of Sukhe Bator, the hero of Mongolian freedom who helped throw off the Manchus some fifty years before. There was a tomb similar to Lenin's, all very impressive by world standards, except for the utter lack of automobiles. A few Russian jeeps such as the one which met us at the airport and a few trucks, that was all.

After much argument with Surén, we convinced him that the outside world, far from feeling the yurt was a blot on the image of new Mongolia, would think it was a beautiful and practical symbol of the country. We pointed out that our own Indians are proud of their heritage and that Americans are trying to preserve the old alongside the new. Whether because of our persuasion or not, we don't know, but Surén did allow us to take pictures of yurts with new concrete office buildings and apartments in the background. For ourselves, we would much rather live in a snug yurt than a cold cement apartment. Yurts are ideal in winter: the smoke hole on top can be cleverly adjusted to temperature, rain, snow or wind by a triangular flap with a rope attached. No cold can get through the heavy felt walls. In the few short summer months, the sides can be rolled up to let a breeze blow through.

A few hours in the museum at Ulan Bator were rewarding; it is a museum to be proud of. Rooms exhibit the history of the Mongols in modern displays, showing the armor of Genghis Khan and Kublai Khan, their way of life, models of the huge yurt drawn by oxen and moved around for the convenience of the khans, carpeted with oriental rugs and luxurious in every detail.

The museum is proud of its display of dinosaur eggs and the complete skeleton of a dinosaur. Mounted animals and birds leave something to be desired, but the same is true of American museums in all but the largest ones.

Even in my wildest imagination, I had never dreamed I would see the famed Gobi Desert. But, before we really knew what was going on, we were whisked again to the airport and boarded on another Ilyushin 14, somewhat battered in appearance but sturdy. Our hostess, a pretty Mongolian girl in sweater, skirt and long wool stockings in shades of red, purple and blue made us feel very comfortable. Again, we noticed the Mongols were smiling, polite and seemingly light-hearted, although it is beyond my imagination how anyone can come out of a Siberian winter with a smile.

We left Ulan Bator on our southbound flight and the woods disappeared abruptly, the country spreading out in a vast panorama of rolling hills and water courses — not necessarily with water in them. The collective farms soon gave way to widely-spaced yurts and herds of bactrian camels, goats, sheep and horses.

A little over an hour later, we came down on gravelly, sod-covered ground and taxied up to a small building. Men riding ponies and camels got out of the way of the plane as we approached. No runway in evidence but the ground was flat and hard. Later we were informed that when it rained, usually in mid-summer, planes couldn't land because of the mud.

A group of onlookers assembled. All were Mongolians with their *dels* in lovely shades of blue and rust and purple, and their sashes in contrasting colors. The women's headscarves were gayly colored and the men's hats an odd shaped assortment.

And then there were the apple-faced, pink-cheeked, bright-eyed children — miniatures of their parents. This was

Dalan Tzadagad, the capital of the South Gobi. A few miles to the east we saw the small town, but we were told we would not be allowed to go into it. We never found out why. Perhaps they thought we might be critical of the large number of yurts surrounding the white concrete buildings that formed the nucleus of the town. We could, however, see them from the air.

In half an hour, we were herded back into the plane — camels, ponies and people shooed off the runway — and took off to the west. In fifteen minutes we landed again on gravel and taxied up to a group of yurts. Not being able to pronounce the name of the place, we called it Yurtville, our home away from home for the next ten days.

Here at last was the famous Gobi Desert — land of the blue sky. To our prejudiced eyes, our own New Mexico sky was really bluer, but we didn't hurt Surĕn's feelings by saying so. The more or less flat grassy plains stretched out to the horizon except in the south where the Altai Mountains jaggedly rose to separate us from China (or Inner Mongolia). One lone distant yurt reminded us of the isolated dome-shaped hogans which our nomadic Navajos still use. An almost incessant wind blew as it does in all the deserts we have ever seen, possibly due to the temperature variation from mountains to desert flats.

Supper was served in a dining yurt, set up with six tables for foreign visitors. The food was adequate but left much to be desired and we (spoiled Americans) were thankful we had brought vitamins along to make up for an almost complete lack of fruits and vegetables. But the tea was excellent, imported from China. We learned to enjoy rice boiled in sheep's milk, but both the mares' milk and the camels' milk were too thick and sweet for our palates.

Mutton was tough and strong, boiled or chopped into a gelatinous consistency. When broiled in shushliks (shishkabobs, Mongolian style) it was quite tasty. As tourists, we sometimes were treated to eggs at breakfast, but they were rare, used only on special occasions. Canned peas, caviar, tiny potatoes the size of walnuts and, once in a while, canned green peaches from North Korea — so sour that we learned to melt some sand-impregnated sugar on them before eating.

Of course, the Mongols practically live on the products of their mares, which they milk, sometimes twice a day. This in itself seemed difficult to us since a colt has to start the milk flowing and even then, only a scant cupful is produced at each milking. Carried in a skin bag and fermented to produce kumiss, this is the same beverage Genghis Khan and his warriors consumed.

Kumiss is supposedly full of life-giving vitamins and perhaps it contributes to the sunny disposition of the Mongolians. Its alcoholic content is not high but continued intake can produce drunkenness. To Frank and the few Americans hunting there, it was distinctly a drawback. Nightly kumiss parties lasted so late that the men were not ready to hunt early in the morning. But life during the winter months must be so grim that perhaps our Mongol friends couldn't help whooping it up during the summer.

As days passed, we became friends with them despite the language barrier. Historically, they had been virtual slaves of the Manchus from the 17th century until 1911 — completely isolated from the world and deliberately kept under control to avoid a recurrence of the days when their warriors swept into Europe conquering everything in their path.

After a period of independence which lasted from 1911 until 1921, the backwash of the Russian Revolution reached into their backward land. Sukhe Bator, the Red Hero, drove out the White Russian army which was nearly as harsh as the Manchus, and established the first truly Communistic country in the world.

We gathered the Mongols still resent their centuries of subjugation by the Manchus. The memory of how the Chinese merchants bled the country, exchanging their livestock and wools for tea, opium and flour at disastrous prices that kept the Mongols under the Manchus' thumbs was still fresh.

On the other hand, the Russians in their own way were developing the country and were helping the Mongols catch up to the 20th century.

Among other things, the Russians drilled water wells in desert areas. We had read prior to our trip that the Mongols were famous for their personal uncleanliness. So it came as a surprise to see their immaculate dress and sanitary preparation of food. Perhaps all these years the lack of cleanliness was merely due to lack of water.

The Russians were also establishing schools, directing large collectives to improve stock raising, building hospitals, flour mills and textile mills. There is even a university in Ulan Bator. Our only sources of information were Surén and our own observations, but we were impressed by the Mongol's independence of spirit as well as their pride in their heritage and their eagerness to learn.

Supper over, we walked out on the desert to watch the vast arc of sky studded with stars, undimmed by city lights. The Altais were still visible in the distance, outlined against the black sky, mysterious and beckoning. But the wind shortened our dreams of the morrow and we welcomed the snug warmth of our candle-lit yurt.

After a breakfast of rice and sheeps milk, tea and scrambled eggs, two battered Russian jeeps drove up. We piled in and soon were bouncing along parallel to the mountains on a gravel track. After some twenty miles, we headed toward the snow-capped peaks and found a yurt at the mouth of a valley leading into the foothills. Here was a herd of mares ready to be milked. The Mongols have no corrals due to the shortage of wood, but the horses are trained to stick together. The mongols keep their colts in a rope corral and this encourages the mares to stick around.

While the drivers and Surén talked to the owner of the yurt, we took out a spotting scope and scanned the mountains. Almost immediately we spied a herd of ibex — one large male outlined against the sky. Beautifully arched horns gave dignity to his majestic stance.

Frank could hardly wait to start up the valley as far as the car could go and to begin our climb on foot, since there were no horses available.

Anyhow, we soon were bumping along the arroyo some half a mile before parking the jeep. Frank was already out of the car and starting up toward the ibex, keeping the steep hillsides and cliffs between him and the watchful eyes of his quarry.

As for me, I felt at home immediately. The vast open

spaces with blue sky above, jagged mountains and the silence of the wilderness reminded me again of New Mexico. The Altais are a very ancient mountain range, without trees but covered with a mat of low-growing grasses, bushes, sagebrush and flowers. It was such an old mountain range that the steep slopes were easily climbable and even the sheer cliffs could be detoured and the summits reached with little trouble. Having no dangerous animals here except possibly the snow leopard, I would be free to explore on my own, so I selected a high peak that promised an all-encompassing view and started climbing. I missed my snowy Samoyed dog who is my companion on such hikes at home. A few enormous vultures and hawks similar to our redtails sailed and circled overhead. Small horned toad-like lizards scuttled away between rocks.

As I worked my way upward, the view stretched out to far horizons; a brilliant red cliff rose above the valley floor. It was not the Flaming Cliffs where Roy Chapman Andrews had discovered the dinosaur eggs, but a similar formation. The red vibrated in the clear air and, as usual in climbing mountains, what seemed to be the summit toward which I headed, proved to be merely a foothill. More and higher ridges appeared as I climbed.

I sat down to glass the mountain and valleys ahead of me. On the next higher ridge, I could see Frank glassing the ibex from a prone position. After studying them for some time, he and Surén crept back out of sight to circle around and get nearer.

The ibex were slowly grazing uphill toward some precipitous cliffs against the skyline. The monarch stood on his lookout motionless. The herd was moving toward a safe vantage point for a noonday siesta.

I sat on my mountain peak dozing in the sun between sessions of searching with my binoculars. Some two hours later I was aroused by a shot. A huge vulture sailed overhead and some kites which reminded me of the hawklike birds which abound in Egypt. Below, some rock conies scampererd between their burrows, their tiny rabbit-like ears flat against their backs. Otherwise, there was little wildlife around.

A while later, I could see the men returning with their

burden down a steep mountainside toward the arroyo where the jeep was parked. I slipped and skidded down the steep rocky mountain arriving at the jeep at the same time as the men. The jeep had just then returned from a kumiss party at the yurt at the entrace to the foothills.

Our return in triumph to Yurtville was hair-raising. Whereas the ancient Mongols took savage delight in racing their ponies — as they still do — our drivers took delight in racing the two jeeps, shouting with glee while we clung to any support available. They sang Mongol songs with gay abandon — songs which were very catchy but hard for our western ears to pick up. We gathered later that they use a five-tone scale and different rhythms, but to us, the effect was not similar to either the Chinese falsetto or to the Russians.

Many times I wished we had had a tape recorder to bring back these rollicking tunes. I did learn one love song from Sumya, a Mongolian girl who often accompanied me to see that nothing untoward happened to me, but it took me several days and lots of practice and, of course, I never could master the guttural language itself. Even the simple "thank you," which sounded like "barirla" with rolling rs but pronounced in the throat, is almost impossible for us to duplicate.

That evening, we were herded into the big Russian bus which was used to bring people and supplies from Dalan Tzadagad. This evening a delegation of Estonians appeared out of nowhere, apparently guests of the Russians, being given an educational tour of Communist countries. A sheet was hung in the front of the jeep and a small noisy gasoline motor outside supplied the power for a motion picture projector. We were shown an excellent color movie, complete with sound, obviously for propaganda purposes. But it was fascinating, showing many parts of Mongolia that we would never be allowed to visit. Not only were the factories and power dams shown, but beautiful forests and waterfalls in the northern section of the country.

On two other nights during our stay when other delegations arrived — Czechs, Japanese Communists and Rumanians — we saw more movies. One was like a Walt Disney feature of the folklore of Mongolia — the plot reminiscent of Hans

Christian Anderson. Here a man had three sons, two wicked and one good, with the ensuing guaranteed results — the good guys always winning in the end. The other movie was mostly musical, singers featured folk songs, a symphony orchestra playing *Carmen* on Mongolian instruments and dressed in gorgeous *dels.* These instruments were very melodious and the music truly beautiful. The foremost was the morin khour, a violin-like affair with the fingerboard ending at the top with a horse's head carved in wood.

Our stay in the Gobi Desert was fascinating; some days were warm as summer and then a wind would arise and the next morning several inches of snow might appear miraculously turning the desert and mountains into a white fairyland. These days were fun since they were not too cold and we could see animal tracks in the snow. Frank nearly tracked down a snow leopard on one of these hunts.

The men took off for a tent camp near the Red Chinese border for a few days. I amused myself riding bactrian camels. Their gait is much smoother than the one-humpers or dromedaries — and riding them without any saddle is quite comfortable. I learned that when their humps are both erect, they are in excellent condition but when a hump wilts, the camel is either tired or undernourished.

Frank finally returned from his hunt with a fine Argali sheep, but he still wanted to get into the main Altais to the west where the sheep are larger and have tremendous horns. The Mongols couldn't understand why we wanted such big horns. They throw them away.

A strong wind blew that night and we feared we were in for a frightful dust storm, for which this region is famous. But lo and behold, in the morning we looked out upon a landscape of glistening snow. The Altais, in their white robes, reminded me of the Alaskan range in vastness and beauty.

The sneezing jeeps were warmed up and by the time we reached the ibex valley of the first hunt, the sunshine had warmed the air and we weren't cold anymore. Frank and Surén headed toward Ikhe Bogdo, some 12,000 feet high, while I climbed to a vantage point and watched the snowy tracks of mice, conies and foxes. After a few hours, the men were lost to sight. But the sun was warm and I found a nice smooth rock to relax on. Again I could watch distant ibex and sheep plus a few herds of horses and camels.

The men came back just before dark, Frank triumphant in having at last seen a herd of enormous rams — too far to shoot, but he knew what he wanted to do the next and last day of our stay.

The men had arranged with the yurt owner to have riding horses the next day. As usual, the Russian jeeps refused to start and had to be pushed before the engines turned over. But eventually they started, coughing in protest. Amazingly, the village men had the horses ready when they arrived at the yurt. I stayed at Yurtville this time, knowing I could not stand a whole day's ride on a Mongolian saddle. I skinned an Argali and salted it for drying.

At dark, Frank and Surén returned. Surén had been afraid to go near Ikhe Bogdo. Mongolians are superstitious and we gathered that the graves of Genghis Khan and some of his warriors were reputed to be on the slopes. So Frank went by himself, shot a huge Argali, skinned the cape himself and brought back the cape and horns to where Surén waited. The horns must have weighed close to 100 pounds. But this meant that Frank had at last collected the world famous Argali ram — the largest to be shot by a foreigner since, roughly, 1898 when an Englishman and his wife had hunted in the western Altais. Roy Chapman Andrews had shot several but only fair-sized specimens. His explorations did not take him into the western part of these mountains — the land of the monster sheep.

As we skinned and wrapped and packed our trophies in burlap sacks, the plane circled and soon was taxiing up to the clustered yurts. We hated to say goodbye to our Mongol friends — not that we could — "Sain bai nu" or "Hello," was about the extent of our learning. However, when you share bumpy jeep rides, picnics on mountain sides and climb and explore together, you feel as if you know one another. There were tears in my eyes as I boarded the plane and waved a last goodbye to Sumya. I never was able to teach her *Red River Valley*, but she didn't mind any more than I minded my inadequacy with her language.

Above: Yurt in the Gobi Desert.

Left: Brownie at entrance to their home away from home - the yurt in the Gobi Desert in what we called "Yurtville."

Opposite Top: A group of Mongols in gorgeously colored native dress.

Opposite Bottom: Frank and Brownie in front of their yurt in the Gobi Desert. Doorways are gaily painted.

As we taxied down the gravel runway and the last of the yurts receded into memory, I wondered if the kumiss really was the secret of their wonderful dispositions.

AFTERWORD

FRANK ON FOOT

AFTERWORD
FRANK ON FOOT

My first years with Frank were a liberal education. On a hike in wild country in the early days he would patiently stop to show me where a coyote had passed, a rabbit had run, a fox had sat down to scratch himself or a deer had broken a twig in passing. After he had pointed it out to me, I'd examine it carefully to see what he meant, but many is the time all I could see was a place in the gravel that seemed rougher than the rest; a footprint that was clear to him was so vague to me that I could not begin to identify the animal that had made it. He could interpret indistinct signs with the sureness of an Indian tracker. Sometimes I thought he was living fifty years too late to make use of his true natural abilities. Frank and Daniel Boone would have been buddies.

I began to realize too, as time passed, that he had an uncanny ability to find archaeological sites. He seemed to know the kind of place prehistoric man would have lived or would have made a hunting camp or where he might have sat to chip flint implements. With a group of students he was usually the first to find the choice bits of information though, of course, there were exceptions.

One of our oldest friends, William S. Fulton, an amateur archaeologist who established the Amerind Foundation and Museum in Dragoon, Arizona, was with us examining a ruin one day and we were all picking up pottery and arrowheads when "Pa" Fulton, as we called him, picked up a beautiful travertine pipe right under Frank's heel as he was walking past it. This pipe is now in the Museum and Pa never failed to point it out when we visited him. Few people have ever made such a prize find when out with Frank.

Many people have remarked about this ability of his — some have been jealous of it, some call it Frank's luck and we, who know Frank well, know that he has an inborn sense of what went where and when.

During the war, Frank was stationed with the Navy in Washington where we rented a home in nearby Chevy Chase. Our daughters once remarked that we now lived in a place where Frank couldn't possibly find anything archaeological. But he did. He found pottery and a prehistoric scraper in our yard and, on a walk along the Potomac River, he located several points and even an ancient living site.

In Africa on several safaris, he discovered prehistoric sites, the artifacts of which we turned over to Dr. Leakey, the world famous authority on ancient man in Africa. I found it difficult to concentrate when, at any moment, a passing lion or rhino might appear from behind a bush.

Frank's walking ability stems from his teen years when he walked all summer long with a burro pack train in the high Sierras of California and across the deserts with an outfit called Three Corner Round. The outfit was founded by a couple named Barrett who, childless, decided that their friends' children were getting too soft and civilized. The Barretts are really the ones who started the now-thriving survival camps. They blazed trails in the Sierras now utilized by the Sierra Club. The burros were roped and broken by the boys themselves. Each boy was assigned to a few burros for the summer and packing, tethering and general caring were his total responsibility. The boys learned to cook with meager rations (the era before freeze-dried food) and to bake bread in a Dutch oven. They had to use blocks and tackles to hoist their burros up and down inaccessible cliffs.

On one of these expeditions they crossed the desert to Nevada from the high Sierras and found all the expected waterholes dry. They lost many baby burros born on the trip and a few old timers, but they finally reached water before it was too late. These walking summers developed Frank's body to a point where, when I married him, he could outwalk and outclimb almost any guide we ever had. Certainly no guide surpassed him.

Frank has spent so much of his life among animals and birds that he really thinks like one. Many summers he collected mammals in various parts of the west for the Cleveland Museum of Natural History. I, being an animal lover and not a hunter, felt sorry for his quarry when he hunted. I felt that game never had much of a chance with Frank on the trail. I well remember the first big buck I saw lying alseep under a tree — a brushy foliaged juniper. Frank, of course, pointed him out to me. It was during a snow storm and I had climbed behind Frank to help carry out another buck he had shot for our winter meat supply. The one he showed me was hidden by heavy branches laden with deepening snow. He must have felt snug and invisible. We stopped, admired him and slipped by so as not to disturb him.

About this time, Frank wrote a hunting story about how he had stalked a big buck, found him asleep and not conscious of Frank's presence. The editor wrote back that he liked the story but that it was not a ''real'' situation — Frank must be exaggerating. The editor did not buy the story. A man has to hunt with Frank to experience his fabulous tracking ability.

Our Sandia Mountains are seven miles east of Albuquerque. They rise in jagged ramparts with charming canyons set inside. While it may be autumn weather down where we live, there are skiers up on top enjoying winter. Thus it was that Frank and I used to spend many weekends hiking up canyons watching deer, following bobcat and coyote tracks and looking for mountain lions. We took our dogs with us — the Springer Spaniel following Frank, the Samoyed staying with me. In the 40s and 50s, the canyons were alive with wild animals. This was before the population explosion turned Albuquerque into a metropolis.

One day we were driving back from Tucson where we had visited our grandchildren when we heard on the radio that a TWA Constellation had crashed into the jagged teeth of the Sandias a few miles east of town. These are rugged bastions thrust up by an ancient geologic uplift which caused the east side of the mountain range to rise in a gradual slope while the west drops into a series of precipitous canyons. Appropriately, they have been named "dragons' teeth."

Frank was able to work the pack horses which awaited him nearly up to the wreck where the rescuers could pack out the dead and their luggage. Another reason why Frank had been called upon was that he had security clearance with the Air Force and one of the passengers was carrying secret data from Los Alamos. Frank retrieved it and TWA rewarded him generously for his help.

Frank and I both believe that the most worthwhile and lasting accomplishment of our lives was the establishment of the exotic animal program in New Mexico. We had long been worried about the future of threatened animals in Africa and Asia. Efforts to preserve these endangered species in their native terrain by sending money and advisers were usually failures.

So, after World War II, we decided to bring certain selected animals to the Southwest and, after appropriate study, release them in the wild in ecological niches where they could survive. During these years, Frank was both Chairman of the Zoo Board and Chairman of the New Mexico State Game Commission, so he had authority to carry out this program. The money was largely furnished by Safari Clubs and sportsmen.

First we worked with the Barbary sheep which we released in the Canadian River Canyon in New Mexico. Now there are over 4,000 Barbaries here where they are virtually extinct in Africa. From Southwest Africa we brought greater kudu and the oryx known as gemsbok. More than 500 gemsbok now roam wild south of White Sands, New Mexico, 200 Siberian ibex near Roy, New Mexico and 300 Iranian ibex in the Florida Mountains. We brought markhors from Afghanistan, red sheep from Iran and Persian gazelles. We hope to keep this program going in the future.

All in all, Frank's most amazing characteristic is his mind. He has a memory so keen I often wonder how he can retain all the information he stores away. In the early days sitting around campfires on excavation digs, Frank would start singing cowboy songs, Spanish songs, old-time and popular numbers — verse after verse without hesitation.

When he was in the Navy during the war, he became aide to Admiral Foy and helped to organize the Army-Navy Staff College. The Joint Chiefs of Staff soon found out about his unusual memory and, without any identification, he was sent to invasion headquarters before an important landing or other maneuver. In his head he would carry all the last minute details and revisions for the invasion. I only learned of these journeys after the war.

As a child in Waterbury, Connecticut, I never found a companion of either sex who was even slightly interested in the out-of-doors, so I relied heavily on my doctor father, from whom I inherited my love of nature. I feel deeply grateful that my parents consented to buy me an Old Town canoe to use on Lake Quassapaug some five miles from town. I would take the trolley to the lake all alone, pull the canoe from under a shelter and paddle all afternoon, watching birds. I was competent in any emergency such as a sudden wind whipping white caps into the canoe or driving me far from the shore.

We were a family who loved picnics in wild places (which still existed in those days just before the 20s) and when we visited my grandparents on their farm near Utica, New York, my father took me fishing in the small creek that ran through the woods — no matter that I caught only suckers while daddy caught trout. Later, he joined a fishing club for men only, so of course, I was excluded. Then, on my first trip west to a ranch in Wyoming, I went on a pack trip through Glacier Park with several school friends and my parents as chaperones. My one and only ambition then was to live in the West.

When I met Frank, I knew I had found someone who shared my love of animals (indeed, neither of us was ever really housebroken) and we trusted them — frequently more than people.

Though I never shared Frank's love of hunting, I shared the wilderness with him by taking movies and later, slides of animals and birds while he hunted. I began to study archaeology in order to help his work, both in the field and at the University.

Over the years, the two of us have covered a lot of ground, none of it wasted and I am grateful to have made some tracks of my own.

I am also grateful to have been able to follow Frank.

INDEX